Junior Dictionary & Thesaurus

First published in 2004 by
Miles Kelly Publishing Ltd
Bardfield Centre, Great Bardfield,
Essex, CM7 4SL

This edition published by Bardfield Press in 2005
Bardfield Press is an imprint of Miles Kelly Publishing Ltd

2 4 6 8 10 9 7 5 3

Editorial Director: Anne Marshall
Senior Editor: Belinda Gallagher
Editorial Assistant: Lisa Clayden
Designer: Louisa Leitao
Production: Estela Boulton

ISBN 1-84236-445-6

Printed in China

British Library Cataloguing-in-Publication Data
A catalogue record for this book is available from the British Library

www.mileskelly.net
info@mileskelly.net

Junior Dictionary & Thesaurus

Cindy Leaney

**BARDFIELD
PRESS**

Junior Dictionary

Your dictionary shows you how to spell words and explains what they mean. It also tells you how to use them. Many words will be familiar – the kind you use every day. Some will be new ones you are just beginning to learn. As you use your dictionary you will find fun things to do and look at. Each letter of the alphabet has its own cartoon, and throughout the book there are puzzles, word games and amazing fact panels.

Definitions
These come after the entry. They explain what the word means.

Example sentences
These sentences follow the definition. They give you an example of the word within a sentence.

Alphabetical order
The words in this book are in alphabetical order. The coloured band along the bottom of every page will tell you which letter of the alphabet you are looking at.

Entries
These are the words in **bold** that you look up. There are more than 1300 entries in your dictionary.

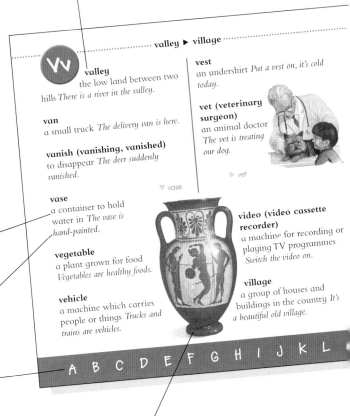

valley ▶ village

valley
the low land between two hills *There is a river in the valley.*

van
a small truck *The delivery van is here.*

vanish (vanishing, vanished)
to disappear *The deer suddenly vanished.*

▼ vase

vase
a container to hold water in *The vase is hand-painted.*

vegetable
a plant grown for food *Vegetables are healthy foods.*

vehicle
a machine which carries people or things *Trucks and trains are vehicles.*

vest
an undershirt *Put a vest on, it's cold today.*

vet (veterinary surgeon)
an animal doctor *The vet is treating our dog.*

▶ vet

video (video cassette recorder)
a machine for recording or playing TV programmes *Switch the video on.*

village
a group of houses and buildings in the country *It's a beautiful old village.*

A B C D E F G H I J K L

Illustrations and photographs
These help you to understand the meaning of a word. Each illustration or photograph has its own label to tell you exactly what it is.

Different forms of a word

Some entries are followed by the same word in plural form. This is when there is more than one of something. Usually this just means adding an 's'. If a plural is more complicated, for example, the plural of 'volcano' is 'volcano**es**', it is shown after the entry within brackets.

inegar
liquid that is used to preserve
od, or add flavour *Put vinegar*
your chips.

iolin
musical instrument that
s played with a bow *My
rother is learning to play
he violin.*

▶ violin

virus (viruses)
1 a very tiny living thing that causes disease and illness *Flu is caused by a virus.*
2 a computer program that can damage files *The virus has damaged my files.*

visit (visiting, visited)
to go to see a person or a place *You can visit us this evening.*

voice
the sounds a person makes when speaking or singing *I didn't recognise your voice.*

volcano (volcanoes)
a mountain with an opening that sprays out steam or lava *The volcano is very active.*

vote (voting, voted)
to show which idea or person you choose by raising your hand or writing on paper *Let's take a vote on this idea.*

How many things can you see beginning with 'v'?

N O P Q R S T U V W X Y Z

If an entry is a verb (doing word) then other forms of the word will appear in brackets. For example, the verb **vote** is followed by different endings.

· Did you know? ·
Look for the orange panels to find out interesting facts about the words in your book.

·Puzzle time·
These are fun things to do and give you a chance to play with words. This helps you to learn and remember them. Puzzle time activities are in green panels.

Cartoons

Look out for the fun cartoons that appear in each letter. How many different things can you see starting with the same letter?

Aa

above

1 in a higher place *Annie lives in the flat above us.*
2 more than *This ride is for children aged six and above.*

accident

something that happens by chance *I dropped it by accident.*

actor (actress, actresses)

a person who plays a part in a film or play *Charlie Chaplin was an actor.*

▶ actor

add (adding, added)

1 to put something together with something else *Add the eggs and sugar.*
2 to put numbers together to find the total *Add six to four to make ten.*

▲ adult

adult

a grown-up, not a child *Only adults are allowed in the pool after six p.m.*

adventure

an exciting experience *Catching the plane by myself was a real adventure.*

advertisement

words or pictures in a newspaper or magazine, or on television or radio, about things for sale *There is an address on the advertisement.*

A B C D E F G H I J K L M

aerial
a piece of metal or wire for receiving or sending radio or television signals *There is an aerial on our roof.*

aeroplane
a large machine, with wings and an engine, that flies *Sometimes aeroplanes fly over our house.*

afraid
a feeling of fear, or that something bad is going to happen *Are you afraid of snakes?*

afternoon
part of the day between midday and the evening *We'll go out this afternoon.*

again
to do something once more *Can you say that again?*

age
the number of years someone has lived *At what age can I learn to drive?*

▼ aeroplane

aircraft
machines that fly *Helicopters, planes and microlights are kinds of aircraft.*

airport
a place where aeroplanes land and take off *The airport is very busy.*

alarm
a machine that flashes or makes a noise as a warning *The burglar alarm is flashing!*

N O P Q R S T U V W X Y Z

alien
something strange that comes from another planet *E. T. is a friendly alien.*

alligator
an animal with a long tail and big teeth that lives around rivers and lakes *Alligators lay eggs.*

alphabet
letters in a special order that form a language *The English alphabet starts with A and ends with Z.*

a b c d e f g h i j k l m n o
p q r s t u v w x y z

ambulance
a vehicle for taking people who are ill or hurt to and from the hospital
Cars pull to one side when an ambulance is coming.

angry
a feeling that something is wrong or unfair *I am angry with you.*

animal
a living thing that can move *Humans, fish, birds and snakes are all animals.*

ankle
part of the body between the leg and the foot that bends *I have twisted my ankle.*

answer
1 something you say or write after a question *My answer is no.*
2 the correct reply to a question or correct result to a problem. *That's the right answer!*

◀ ambulance

A B C D E F G H I J K L M

answer (answering, answered)
1 to say or write something when asked a question *You must answer the questions.*
2 to pick up the telephone or go to the door *Answer the door!*

ant
an insect that lives in groups *There is a line of ants marching into the sugar bowl!*

appear (appearing, appeared)
1 to look or to seem *She appears to be much better.*
2 to come into sight *Our sister suddenly appeared.*

apple
a fruit that grows on trees *Apples are red, yellow or green.*

▶ apple

apricot
a small, fuzzy-skinned yellow fruit *I like dried apricots on cereal.*

apron
a piece of cloth that you put on top of your clothes to keep them clean. *Put an apron on before you open the paint tin.*

▲ How many things can you see beginning with 'a'?

aquarium
a plastic or glass box filled with water for keeping fish in *The fish swim in the aquarium.*

argue (arguing, argued)
to strongly disagree *Don't argue, it's not important.*

arm
the part of your body that is positioned between your shoulder and hand *My right arm is stronger than my left arm.*

armchair
a chair that has places for you to rest your arms *I like to read when I'm sitting in an armchair.*

army
the people that fight for a country on land *The ancient Roman army was very powerful.*

arrest (arresting, arrested)
to take someone away and guard them *The police arrested two people.*

art
the making of paintings, drawings and sculpture *There is an art show at school.*

artist
a person who makes art *Picasso was a famous artist.*

 artist

ask (asking, asked)
to say to someone you want them to tell you something, or do something for you *You should ask for help.*

asleep
sleeping *Shhh, please be quiet, the baby is fast asleep.*

A B C D E F G H I J K L M

astronaut
a person who travels into space in a spacecraft *Astronauts sometimes spend months on a space station.*

athlete
a person who plays a sport *Athletes train every day.*

▶ athlete

attack (attacking, attacked)
to be violent *Pirates attacked the ship.*

aunt
the sister of your mother or father, the wife of your uncle *My aunt looks like my mother.*

autograph
the name of a famous person, written by them *Can I have your autograph?*

automatic
a machine that works by itself *The washing machine is automatic.*

autumn
the time of year between the summer and the winter *The leaves turn red in autumn.*

awake
not sleeping, not asleep *I tried to stay awake all night.*

awful
very bad *This medicine tastes awful.*

axe
a tool with a handle and a sharp piece of metal at the end that is used for chopping wood and cutting down trees *Dad uses an axe to chop wood.*

▶ axe

N O P Q R S T U V W X Y Z

Bb

baboon
a large monkey
Baboons are very noisy.

▼ baby

baby (babies)
a young child that has not yet learned to talk or walk
The baby's name is Alex.

back
1 part of your body behind you, between your shoulders and hips *I can swim on my back.*
2 the part of something that is furthest from the front or from the way it is facing *The wires are at the back of the computer.*

backwards
the direction opposite to the way something is facing *Take four steps backwards.*

bacon
meat from a pig *We have bacon and eggs for breakfast.*

bad (worse, worst)
not good or pleasant *It's bad news.*

badge
a piece of paper, plastic, metal or cloth that you put on your clothes to say who you are or what you have done *I have four swimming badges.*

▶ badger

badger
an animal with black and white fur that lives underground
There is a family of badgers living in the wood.

badly
not done well *I play the piano badly.*

A B C D E F G H I J K L M

badminton

a game such as tennis that is played with rackets and a small object with feathers *We play badminton every day.*

bag

a container made of plastic, paper, cloth or leather *Put the vegetables into one bag.*

baggy

loose, not tight *I like baggy sweaters.*

bake (baking, baked)

to cook food in an oven *Bake the cake for 40 minutes.*

balcony

an area outside a window where you can sit or stand *You can see the beach from the balcony.*

bald

without hair *My dad is going bald.*

ball

an object that you throw, hit or kick in games *Throw the ball in the air.*

ballet

a type of dancing that tells a story with no words *A very famous ballet is* Swan Lake.

balloon

a rubber bag filled with air that is used as a decoration *We had balloons at the party.*

banana

a long, curved yellow fruit *I like bananas for breakfast.*

 bananas

bang

a sudden loud noise *The door shut with a bang.*

N O P Q R S T U V W X Y Z

bank

1 a place to keep money *There is a bank in the town.*
2 the land alongside a river *People sit on the bank and fish.*

▲ How many things can you see beginning with 'b'?

barn

a farm building for keeping animals or crops *The cows are in the barn.*

basket

a container made of thin strips, to hold or carry things *Put the bread in the basket.*

basketball

a game played by two teams who try to get points by throwing a ball through a round net *Basketball is a fast game.*

bat

1 a small animal that usually flies at night *Bats have good hearing.*
2 the wooden stick used to hit a ball in games such as baseball and cricket *Baseball bats are rounded, cricket bats are flat.*

bath

a long container that you fill with water and sit in to wash your body *There's nothing more relaxing than a warm bath at the end of the day.*

beach (beaches)

the area of land that is right next to the sea *Would you like to come for a picnic on the beach?*

A B C D E F G H I J K L M

bean

the seed of a climbing plant that is eaten as food *I like baked beans on toast.*

▶ bear

bear

a large, strong wild animal that is covered in fur *Bears have long, sharp claws.*

beard

hair that grows on a man's chin and cheeks *My Dad has a beard.*

beautiful

very pleasant *Roses are beautiful.*

bed

a piece of furniture for sleeping on *There are two beds in my room.*

bee

a yellow and black striped insect *Bees live in a nest called a hive.*

•Puzzle time•

Untangle the bees to see which one gets home

begin (beginning, began)

to start *Begin at the top of the page.*

behind

at the back of someone or something *She's hiding behind the garden fence.*

N O P Q R S T U V W X Y Z

bell
1 a hollow, metal object that makes a sound when hit *Press the bell for service.*
2 a machine that makes a ringing sound *The bell rings at 3:15 p.m.*

below
in a lower place than something else *The gym is on the floor below.*

belt
a piece of clothing that you wear around your waist *Belts can be made of leather, cloth or plastic.*

bench (benches)
a seat for two or more people to sit on *Wait on the bench.*

better (best)
something of a higher standard or quality *The new game is better than the last one.*

between
in a place or time that separates two things or people *You can sit between us.*

handlebars ▼ bike
saddle
wheel
pedal
chain

bicycle (bike)
a machine with two wheels that you sit on and move by pushing on pedals to make the wheels go round *I'd like a new bicycle for my birthday.*

big (bigger, biggest)
1 large, not small *The shirt is too big.*
2 important *Tomorrow is a big day.*

A B C E D F G H I J K L M

bird
an animal that has
wings, feathers and lays
eggs *Most birds
can fly.*

▶ bird

birthday
the day of the year on which a
person is born *When is your birthday?*

biscuit
a dry, thin cake that is usually sweet
Would you like a biscuit?

bite (biting, bit, bitten)
to cut into something
with your teeth
*Have a bite of
the apple.*

▶ bite

bitter
having a strong, sharp taste such
as coffee *Add sugar, it tastes bitter.*

blanket
a piece of material on a bed that
you use to keep warm *There's a
blanket on the bed.*

blind
not able to see *Talking books are made
for blind people.*

blister
a raised piece of skin, filled with
liquid, caused by burning or rubbing
I have a blister on my foot.

blizzard
a very heavy snow storm
*People shouldn't drive in a
blizzard.*

blood
liquid that the heart
pumps through your
body *The colour of blood
is dark red.*

N O P Q R S T U V W X Y Z

bloom (blooming, bloomed)
to open out into a flower *There are flowers blooming all over the garden.*

blow (blowing, blew)
to push air out of your mouth *It's fun to blow bubbles!*

boat
a small ship *You get to the island by boat.*

body (bodies)
1 the whole of a person *Skin covers your body.*
2 a dead person *They covered the body with a blanket.*

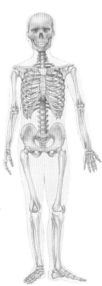

▶ bones

bone
a hard, white part under the skin of a person or animal *Your skeleton has more than 200 bones.*

book
1 sheets of paper with writing on, joined together for reading *This is a book about spiders.*
2 sheets of paper joined together for writing on *Write your name on the cover of your exercise book.*

boot
1 a shoe that covers your foot and ankle *Wear your boots in the rain.*
2 part of a car for carrying things *The bags are in the boot.*

▲ boots

bored
not interested *I'm bored, let's play a game.*

born
to start life *When were you born?*

A **B** C D E F G H I J K L M

borrow (borrowing, borrowed)
to have something that belongs to another person and return it to them *You can borrow the books for two weeks.*

bottle
a tall container for storing liquid *I have a water bottle on my bike.*

▶ bottles

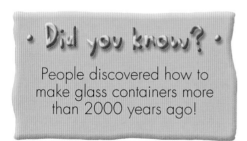

• **Did you know?** •
People discovered how to make glass containers more than 2000 years ago!

bottom
the lowest part of something *The number is at the bottom of the page.*

bounce (bouncing, bounced)
1 to move back quickly after hitting or falling on something *Bounce on the trampoline.*
2 to throw an object against something so it moves back quickly *Bounce the ball against the wall.*

bow
1 a knot with loops *Tie a bow on top of the present.*
2 a long, thin stick with string for shooting arrows or playing an instrument *You play the violin with a bow.*

bow (bowing, bowed)
to bend your body or your head to show respect *The servants all bowed to the king.*

bowl
a deep, curved dish *You eat cereal out of a bowl.*

N O P Q R S T U V W X Y Z

box (boxes)
a container with four sides *Keep the crayons in a box.*

boxing
the sport of fighting with closed hands *There is a boxing match on TV.*

boy
a male child or a young man *There are two boys in their family.*

bracelet
a piece of jewellery worn around the wrist *My bracelet has my name on it.*

brain
the part of your body inside your head that you use for thinking, feeling and moving *When you touch something hot, nerves send a message to your brain and you pull your hand away.*

branch
the part of a tree that grows out from the trunk *Leaves, flowers and fruit grow on branches.*

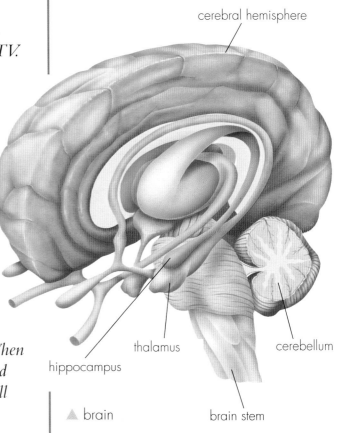

cerebral hemisphere

thalamus

hippocampus

cerebellum

brain stem

▲ brain

A B C D E F G H I J K L M
▲

bread
a type of food made with flour, water and yeast *Have some bread.*

break (breaking, broke, broken)
to make something separate into two or more pieces *I've broken a glass.*

breakfast
the first meal of the day *We had cereal for breakfast.*

breeze
a light wind *There's a breeze blowing.*

brick
a block of baked clay used for building *The wall is made from bricks.*

bridge
a structure built to join two things *There is a bridge over the river.*

▶ bridge

bright
1 full of light *It's a bright, sunny day.*
2 strong and easy to see *Wear bright colours when you go into the forest.*
3 clever, intelligent *That's a bright idea.*

brilliant
1 very bright and strong *The North Star is brilliant.*
2 very good at doing something *She's a brilliant scientist.*
3 very good or enjoyable *It's a brilliant game!*

N O P Q R S T U V W X Y Z

bring (bringing, brought)
to take something with you *Why don't you come over tonight and bring a friend with you?*

broccoli
a green vegetable *Let's have broccoli with our dinner.*

broom
a brush with a handle *Sweep the floor with a broom.*

brother
a boy or a man who has the same parents as another person *Nadia has two brothers.*

brush (brushes)
a tool that has stiff hairs fastened to a handle that is used for sweeping, painting, cleaning or smoothing *It's always best to wash your paintbrushes in cold water.*

bucket
a round, open container with a handle *Put the water in a bucket.*

build (building, built)
to make something, such as a house, by putting pieces together *There are plans to build a new school next year.*

·Puzzle time·

Which of these brushes is the odd one out?

answer:
broom

A B C D E F G H I J K L M

building

a man-made place, usually with a roof and walls *The Taj Mahal is a building in India.*

▶ building

bull

a male cow, elephant or whale *There's a bull running loose in that field.*

burglar

a person who goes into buildings to steal things *A burglar stole the money.*

burn (burning, burned, burnt)

1 to be on fire *The candles are burning.* **2** to destroy something with fire *The shed burnt down.*

bus (buses)

a vehicle that carries passengers *The bus stops at our road.*

bush (bushes)

a small tree *Berries grow on bushes.*

butter

yellow food that is made from milk *Spread butter on the bread.*

butterfly (butterflies)

an insect with large wings *Butterflies drink from flowers.*

◀ butterfly

button

a round object that fastens clothes *The dress has one button.*

buy (buying, bought)

to get something by paying money for it *Shall we buy some sweets?*

N O P Q R S T U V W X Y Z

▶ cabbage

cabbage

a large vegetable with thick, round leaves *Rabbits love eating cabbages.*

cabin

1 a small house made of wood, usually in the country *The cabin is halfway up the mountain.*
2 the place where the passengers sit inside an aeroplane *The pilot walked back through the cabin.*
3 a small room to sleep in on a ship *The cabin has two beds.*

cactus (cacti, cactuses)

a plant that grows in hot, dry places that has needles instead of leaves *The needles on a cactus are sharp.*

▶ cactus

café

a place that serves drinks and simple meals *Why don't we stop and have lunch at a café?*

cage

a room or box made of bars in which to keep animals or birds *Pet hamsters and mice live in cages.*

cake

a sweet food made of flour, sugar and eggs that is baked in an oven *Mum baked me a chocolate cake for my birthday.*

calendar

a special chart that shows the days, weeks and months of the year *We wrote everyone's birthday on the calendar.*

A B C D E F G H I J K L M

calf (calves)
1 a baby cow, elephant or whale
The calf is two days old.
2 the back part of your leg between
your ankle and knee *I've pulled a
muscle in my calf.*

▼ calf

call (calling, called)
1 to shout or say something in a
loud voice *Dad calls us in for dinner at
six o'clock.*
2 to telephone *Call me when you get
home.*
3 to visit *The doctor calls when someone
is very ill.*
4 to give someone or something a
name *They called the baby Luke.*

camel
a large animal with one
or two humps that can
carry heavy loads *A camel
can go without water for a long
time.*

▶ camel

camera
a piece of equipment used for taking
photographs or filming *You get a
digital camera free with this computer.*

camp
a place where people stay in tents
The camp is over the hill.

camp (camping, camped)
to stay in a tent *Every summer the
scouts camp in this field.*

can
a metal container *We collect drink
cans for charity.*

N O P Q R S T U V W X Y Z

can (could)

1 to be able to do something *Aziz can use the Internet.*
2 to be allowed to do something *We can come to your party.*

▶ candle

candle

a stick of wax with a string through it that you burn for light *There are nine candles on her birthday cake.*

captain

1 someone who leads a team *Who is captain of the football team this year?*
2 a person who is in charge of a ship or a plane *The captain says the flight will take two hours.*

▶ car

car

a machine on wheels that has an engine and that people can ride in *There is a car in the driveway.*

caravan

a small house on wheels that can be pulled behind a car *David and Katya have taken the caravan on holiday.*

card

1 thick, stiff paper *Use a piece of card to make a sign from.*
2 a piece of card with words and a picture that you give or send someone *My brother gave me a birthday card to open.*
3 a piece of stiff paper or plastic that you use to buy things or to identify yourself *I have a library card.*
4 a piece of stiff paper with pictures and numbers that you use to play games *Give each player seven cards.*

A B C D E F G H I J K L M

cardigan
a piece of clothing such as a sweater with buttons down the front *Wear a cardigan if it's cold.*

careful (carefully)
paying attention to what you are doing so that you don't make a mistake or have an accident *Be careful! That knife is sharp.*

carpet
a thick cover for the floor *The carpet in my bedroom is green and blue.*

carrot
a long, orange vegetable that grows under the ground *Carrots are a very healthy food to eat.*

carry (carrying, carried)
to move something from one place to another *Can you help me carry all the shopping indoors?*

cassette
a plastic box with a tape inside it for recording or playing back sound or video *Put the cassette into the stereo.*

castle
a large, strong building with thick walls *Castles were built to keep the people inside safe from their enemies.*

· **Did you know?** ·
Berkeley Castle is said to be haunted by the ghost of King Edward II.

▶ cat

cat
a small, furry animal with a long tail and sharp claws *My cat likes to climb trees.*

catch (catching, caught)
1 to get hold of something *Catch the ball!*
2 to get an illness *People often catch cold in winter.*
3 to get on a bus, train, plane or ferry and go somewhere *We usually catch the bus to the airport.*

▲ How many things can you see beginning with 'c'?

caterpillar
an animal, like a worm with legs, that turns into a butterfly or a moth *Caterpillars eat leaves.*

cave
a hole in a mountainside or under the ground *Caves are usually dark.*

CD (CDs, compact disc)
a circular piece of plastic for storing sound *Have you bought their latest CD? It's really good!*

CD-ROM (CD-ROMs, compact disc read-only memory)
a circular piece of plastic for storing information to be used by a computer *CD-ROMs hold lots of information.*

celery
a vegetable that is often used in salads *Celery is crunchy.*

cereal
a breakfast food that is made from plants such as wheat, oats and rice *Pour some milk on the cereal.*

chair
a piece of furniture for sitting on *Pull your chair close to the desk.*

A B C D E F G H I J K L M

chalk
a soft, white rock *We used different coloured chalk to draw the picture.*

chameleon
a lizard that changes colour so its skin matches the things around it *Chameleons eat flies.*

change (changing, changed)
1 to become different or to make something different *You haven't changed at all!*
2 to put on different clothes *I'll be downstairs as soon as I've changed into something warmer.*

cheap (cheaper, cheapest)
not expensive *This watch is cheap but it is well-made.*

cheese
a food that is made from milk *Can I have some cheese on toast for supper?*

cherry (cherries)
a small, round reddish fruit that has a stone in the centre *We'll have cherry pie for dessert.*

▲ cherries

chest
1 the part of your body between your neck and your stomach *Place the belt across your chest.*
2 a strong box with a top that locks *The chest was filled with gold!*

chicken
a farm bird that is kept for eggs and meat *Chickens can't fly very far.*

child (children)
1 a young person *He's just a child.*
2 someone's son or daughter *They love all their children.*

chimney
an opening over a fire that takes smoke out through the roof of a building *The chimney is filled with soot.*

chin
part of your face under your mouth *His beard hides his chin.*

chips
pieces of potato fried in oil *Do you like fish and chips?*

chocolate
a sweet food made from cocoa beans *Would you like some chocolate?*

Christmas
a Christian holiday *Where are you spending Christmas?*

▶ circus

church (churches)
the place where Christians meet to worship *The church is full of flowers.*

cinema
a place you go to see films *Shall we go to the cinema?*

circus (circuses)
a show with people and animals, held in a big tent *The circus is in town!*

city (cities)
a large town *It is a big, busy city.*

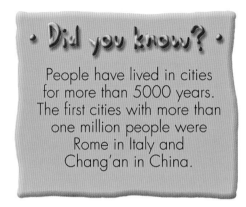

• Did you know? •
People have lived in cities for more than 5000 years. The first cities with more than one million people were Rome in Italy and Chang'an in China.

clap (clapping, clapped)
to make a loud sound by hitting the palms of your hands together *The actors bowed and we clapped louder.*

class (classes)
1 a group of people who learn together *We're in the same class.*
2 a group of things or animals that are the same *People belong to the class of animals called mammals.*

claw
a sharp, hard part of an animal's foot *Cats have sharp claws.*

clean
not dirty *The car is clean and shiny.*

clean (cleaning, cleaned)
to make something tidy, to take dirt away *Clean your room!*

clear
1 easy to understand, hear or read *The instructions are clear.*
2 easy to see through *You can see the fish swimming in the clear water.*

clever
able to learn or understand things quickly *Well done – you're very clever.*

cliff
the side of a rock or mountain *The road runs along a cliff.*

climb (climbing, climbed)
to move upwards *She climbed to the top.*

clock
a machine that tells the time *The clock said 5:55 a.m.*

close
near *The hotel is close to the beach.*

▶ clock

close (closing, closed)
to shut *Close the window, I'm cold.*

cloth
1 a soft material *The chair is covered in cloth.*
2 a piece of cloth for a special purpose *Clean the window with a cloth.*

clothes
things that people wear *Shirts, jeans and skirts are all clothes.*

cloud
a white or grey object in the sky that is made of tiny drops of water *It's a beautiful day, just a few clouds.*

clown
someone who makes people laugh *Harry is our class clown.*
▶ clown

coast
the land next to the sea *The village is on the coast.*

coat
a piece of clothing you wear over your clothes to stay warm or keep the rain off *This is a warm coat.*

A   B   **C**   D   E   F   G   H   I   J   K   L   M
▲

coconut
the nut of the palm tree *Coconuts give delicious juice.*

cocoon
the bag around an insect that protects it while it is growing into an adult *The cocoon broke open and a butterfly flew out.*

coffee
the brown beans of a plant, or a hot drink that can be made from them *I'm making a hot drink, would you prefer tea or coffee?*

coin
a piece of money that is made of metal *They keep coins from their holidays.*

cold
not warm or hot *Brrr – this water is very cold.*

collect (collecting, collected)
to put things together in one place *Some people collect coins.*

▲ colour

colour
blue, green, red or yellow *What colour is your jacket?*

colour (colouring, coloured)
to make something a colour with paint, crayons or ink *We coloured the picture in.*

comb
an object for making your hair tidy *Don't let anyone use your comb.*

N O P Q R S T U V W X Y Z

comic

a magazine with pictures that tell a story *Comics are often funny.*

compass

an object that shows you what direction you are travelling in *Read the compass to find the treasure!*

▲ compass

competition

a test to see who is best at something *There was a singing competition on the radio.*

complain (complaining, complained)

to say that something is wrong and you are not happy about it *He complained to the waiter.*

computer

a machine for storing information and doing jobs such as sums and writing letters *You can play games on computers.*

confused

a feeling of not being sure *I was confused by the question.*

container

something that holds something else in it *Jars, tins and boxes are containers.*

cook

to make food hot so it can be eaten *Ahmed is cooking dinner for us.*

cool

a little bit cold *There is a cool breeze.*

copy (copying, copied)

to do something the same as something else *Copy the writing.*

A B C D E F G H I J K L M
▲

corn
1 a plant with large, yellow seeds
This corn is delicious.
2 the seeds of plants such
as wheat and oats
*Many farmers grow
different types of corn
every year.*

 corn

**cough
(coughing, coughed)**
to force air from your throat *She's
still coughing, give her a drink of water.*

count (counting, counted)
to find out how many *Count the
children in the playground.*

▶ crab

country (countries)
1 a place with its own government
Which country do you live in?
2 away from cities and towns *We live
in a village in the country.*

cousin
the child of your aunt or uncle
Charlie is my cousin.

cow (cattle, cows)
a large, female farm animal that
gives milk *Cows eat grass.*

cowboy
a man who rides a horse and takes
care of cattle *The cowboy tried to ride
the horse.*

crab
a sea animal that moves
sideways and has big
claws *Crabs are good
to eat.*

N O P Q R S T U V W X Y Z

crack
where something is broken *There's a crack in this mug.*

crack (cracking, cracked)
to break something so that a line appears on it *Just crack the shell.*

crash (crashing, crashed)
1 to have an accident *The car crashed into a tree.*
2 to make a loud noise *Hear the thunder crash!*

crawl (crawling, crawled)
to move around on your hands and knees
The baby is starting to crawl.

crayon
a coloured wax stick *Can I use your crayons?*

creep (creeping, crept)
to move so that no one sees or hears you *Oh! Don't creep up on me!*

crisps
fried, thin slices of potato *I love eating crisps.*

crocodile
a large animal with a long body, short legs and big teeth that lives in rivers and lakes *Crocodiles live in hot countries.*

crooked
not straight *The fence is very crooked.*

◄ crocodile

crop
plants that are grown for people and animals to eat, or that are used to make things *The weather is very important to farmers who grow crops.*

A B C D E F G H I J K L M

cross
two lines that go over each other
There is a cross on the map where the treasure is hidden.

cross (crossing, crossed)
to go from one side of
something to the
other *Cross the road
carefully.*

▶ crown

crown
a metal circle that
kings and queens wear
on their heads *The queen and king
are both wearing gold crowns.*

cruel
not kind *He's a cruel king.*

crumb
A small piece of something such as
bread or cake *Whose eaten the cake?
There are only crumbs left.*

cry (crying, cried)
1 to make tears from your eyes,
usually because you feel sad or are
hurt *Sometimes you feel better after you
have cried.*
2 to shout *"Help! Help!" they cried.*

cucumber
a long, thin green vegetable that is
used in salads *I'd like a cucumber and
tomato salad.*

cuddle (cuddling, cuddled)
to hold someone in your arms to
show you care *Chloe cuddled her best
friend to cheer her up.*

▶ cuddle

N O P Q R S T U V W X Y Z

cup
a container with a handle for drinking from *Put a teabag in the cup, then add water.*

cupboard
a piece of furniture for storing things *Please dry the dishes and put them in the cupboard.*

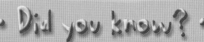

Did you know?
Hair grows from a follicle (pit) in the scalp. Coloured substances called melanin (dark brown) and carotene (yellowish) give hair its colour. Black, curly hair is the result of black melanin growing from a flat follicle.

curious
wanting to know or find out about something *Cats are very curious.*

curl
something like hair or ribbon that is curved at the end *She has beautiful curls.*

▶ curls

curtain
cloth that hangs across or over a window *Pull the curtains at night.*

cushion
a bag with soft material inside for sitting or lying on *Put a cushion under your head.*

cut (cutting, cut)
to remove something with a knife or scissors *I'm going to get my hair cut.*

Dd

daisy (daisies)
a flower with white petals and a yellow centre *You can make a chain of daisies.*

dance (dancing, danced)
to move your body to music *This music is good to dance to.*

dangerous
not safe *Playing with matches is dangerous.*

dark
not light *It's too dark to play outside.*

daughter
a female child *My daughter isn't well.*

day
1 a 24-hour period *We're staying for three days.*
2 from the time the sun rises until it sets *Bats do not fly during the day.*

▲ daisies

dead
not alive *This plant looks dead.*

deaf
not able to hear *Many deaf people can read lips.*

dear
1 a word to start a letter *Dear Aran, How are you?*
2 much cared about *She's a very dear friend.*
3 expensive *The dress is too dear.*

deep

a long way from the top to the bottom, or from the front to the back *I'm not afraid to swim in the deep end of the pool.*

deer (deer)

an animal that lives in forests *Deer are gentle animals.*

delicious

tasting very good *This ice cream is delicious.*

delighted

very happy *I'm delighted with my new bike.*

▶ dessert

dentist

a person who looks after people's teeth *I go to the dentist twice a year.*

desert

a place where there is very little or no rain *Most deserts are hot.*

desk ▲ desert

a piece of furniture that you sit at to read, write or use a computer *There's a lamp on my desk.*

dessert

sweet food that you eat at the end of a meal *What's for dessert?*

detective

a person who finds information about a crime or another person *Some police officers are detectives.*

A B C D E F G H I J K L M

diary

a book with the days of the year in it that you use to write down what you plan to do, or what you have done *I write in my diary before I go to bed each night.*

die (dice)

a cube with spots on each side that is used for playing games *It's your turn – throw the dice.*

die (dying, died)

to stop living *Water the plant before it dies.*

different

not the same *These two sweets look the same but they taste different.*

difficult

not easy *I hope the spelling test isn't too difficult.*

dig (digging, dug)

to make a hole in the earth or to move it *Big machines can dig faster than we can.*

▶ digger

digital

1 showing information using numbers that can change *This is a digital watch.*
2 storing information using only zero and one *Most music is digitally recorded these days.*

dining room

the room in which you eat your meals *The dining room is next to the kitchen in our house.*

N O P Q R S T U V W X Y Z

dinner

the main evening meal *What's for dinner?*

dinosaur

an animal that became extinct 65 million years ago *One type of dinosaur was* Tyrannosaurus Rex.

dirty

not clean, messy *We put dirty clothes in the washing basket.*

disabled

a disabled person cannot use part of their body *This parking space is for disabled drivers only.*

disappear (disappearing, disappeared)

to go out of sight or become impossible to find *The sun disappeared behind a cloud.*

disco

a place or a party where people dance *There's a disco on Saturday.*

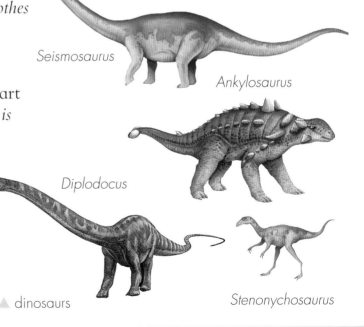

Seismosaurus

Ankylosaurus

Stegosaurus

Diplodocus

Stenonychosaurus

▲ dinosaurs

A B C D E F G H I J K L M

discover (discovering, discovered)
to find or understand something for the first time *Alexander Fleming discovered penicillin, a type of medicine.*

disease
a serious illness *Flu is a disease.*

disguise
something that you wear to hide who you really are *He's in disguise.*

dish (dishes)
something like a bowl or plate, used for serving food *Please dry the dishes.*

disk
a piece of plastic for storing computer information *Save the file on a disk.*

dive (diving, dived)
to go into water headfirst *I can dive.*

dizzy
the feeling that things are turning around you or that you are going to fall *That ride makes me dizzy.*

doctor
a person who looks after sick people or helps stop people from being ill *Doctors work very hard.*

▶ doctor

document
1 papers that contain official information *Important documents are filed away.*
2 a piece of work that is saved in a file on a computer *You can attach a document to an email.*

dog
an animal that people keep as a pet
Our dog is a sheep dog.

doll
a toy in the shape of a person *Let's play with our dolls.*

dolphin
a large, warm-blooded animal that lives in the ocean *A dolphin looks like a fish but it is an air-breathing mammal.*

domino (dominoes)
a piece of black wood or plastic with white spots that is used to play games *Playing dominoes is good for your maths!*

donkey
an animal that looks similar to a small horse with a long tail and big ears *Every day we feed carrots to the donkeys near our house.*

door
something that you open and close to go into or out of a room, house or car *Can you open the door for me?*

down
1 towards a lower place *Get down off the ladder.*
2 at a lower rate or speed *Prices are coming down.*

dragon
▼ dragon
an imaginary animal such as a big lizard that breathes fire *The story is about a princess trapped in a dragon's cave.*

dramatic
surprising or exciting *It's dramatic news.*

A B C D E F G H I J K L M

draw (drawing, drew, drawn)
to make a picture *You can draw well.*

drawer
part of a piece of furniture that slides in and out that is used for storing things *Put all the clothes in the drawer.*

dream (dreaming, dreamt or dreamed)
1 to think about or see things in your sleep *I dreamed that I could fly.*
2 to hope for something *We dream of being famous.*

dress (dressing, dressed)
to put clothes on *Get dressed, we're ready to go.*

dress (dresses)
a piece of clothing for girls or women that has a top and skirt *That's a beautiful dress.*

drink
liquid food *Would you like a drink?*

drink (drinking, drank, drunk)
to take liquid into your mouth and swallow it *Drink lots of water.*

◀ drink

drive (driving, drove, driven)
to control a vehicle, such as a car *My oldest brother can drive.*

drop (dropping, dropped)
to fall or to let something fall *Don't drop that vase.*

N O P Q R S T U V W X Y Z

▶ drum

drum

a musical instrument that you hit with a stick or your hand *He plays the drums.*

• Did you know? •

Giant drums are used in the temple ceremonies of Japan's oldest religion, Shinto. The largest drum measures 1.8 metres across and weighs 4 tonnes.

dry

not wet *The washing is nearly dry.*

duck

a bird with webbed feet that lives near water *We feed bread to the ducks.*

▲ How many things can you see beginning with 'd'?

dustbin

a big container for storing rubbish *The dustbins are emptied on Tuesdays.*

DVD (digital versatile disk)

a circular piece of plastic used for storing and playing music and films *Is the film on DVD?*

A B C D E F G H I J K L M

Ee

eagle
a bird that hunts for its food *An eagle has sharp claws called talons.*

ear
the part of your body that you use to hear *My ears feel cold.*

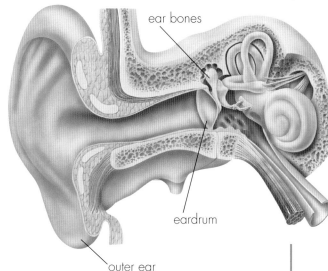

ear bones

eardrum

outer ear

early
before the normal time *I wake up early in the summer.*

earn (earning, earned)
to get money for work *I earn extra pocket money for washing the car.*

earring
a piece of jewellery that is worn on the ear *Can I wear my new earrings?*

◀ ear

Earth (earth)
1 the planet we live on *Earth travels around the Sun.*
2 soil *Sprinkle earth over the seeds.*

earthquake
a strong shaking of the earth *Earthquakes can cause serious damage.*

Easter
a Christian holiday *We're spending Easter at home.*

N O P Q R S T U V W X Y Z

easy
not difficult *This book is easy to read.*

eat (eating, ate, eaten)
to take food into your mouth and swallow it *What shall we have to eat?*

echo (echoes)
a sound that bounces off something and can be heard again *There is a strong echo when you shout into the cave.*

▶ eggs

egg
1 an oval object with a shell that some animals lay, from which their babies hatch *The robin has laid an egg.*
2 an egg used as food *Shall we make fried eggs for breakfast?*

elbow
where your arm bends *Ouch, I bumped my elbow.*

electricity
power that is used to make lights and machines work *Lightning is a giant spark of electricity.*

elephant
a large, wild animal with a long nose called a trunk *A baby elephant is called a calf.*

email
messages sent by computer *I received emails from all my friends.*

empty
with nothing inside *The box is empty.*

end
to finish or stop *The film ends at 6:30 p.m.*

A B C D E F G H I J K L M

enemy (enemies)
someone who does not like you, or wants to hurt you *We are enemies, not friends.*

energy
strength or power *We're trying to save energy.*

engine
1 a machine that makes something work *Most engines are in the front of cars.*
2 Part of a train that pulls the other carriages *The steam engine is very noisy.*

enjoy (enjoying, enjoyed)
to like to do something *I enjoy playing tennis.*

enormous
very, very big *Whales are enormous animals.*

enough
as much as you need *There is enough for everyone.*

enter (entering, entered)
1 to go into a place *The king entered the hall.*
2 to put information into a computer *The names and addresses are entered in a file.*

◀ engine

N O P Q R S T U V W X Y Z

entrance
the way into a place *The entrance to the cave was very dark.*

envelope
a paper cover for letters and cards *Put a stamp on the envelope.*

▶ envelopes

environment
everything around us, such as land, air or water *They live in a hot environment.*

equal
the same as something else in number, size or amount *One kilogram is equal to 1000 grams.*

equipment
things that are used to do something such as work or sport *Our school has lots of new computer equipment.*

escalator
a staircase that moves *We went up the escalator.*

escape (escaping, escaped)
to leave a place that is dangerous or unpleasant *They escaped from the prison.*

evening
the time of day between afternoon and night time *It starts to get dark in the evening.*

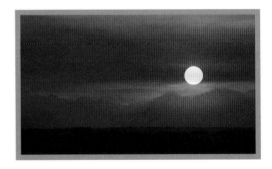

▲ evening

excellent
very good *This is an excellent song.*

A B C D E F G H I J K L M

excited
happy and interested in something
I am excited about tomorrow.

excuse
a reason you give for something
that you have said or done *Her
excuse for being late is that she overslept.*

exercise
movements that you make to stay fit
and healthy *Exercise keeps you fit.*

exhibition
a show where people can look at
things like paintings *There is an
exhibition of our artwork at school.*

exit
the way to leave a place *There is a
light over the exit.*

expensive
costing a lot *Jewellery can be expensive.*

explain (explaining, explained)
to say what something means or
why it has happened *Our teacher
explained how the equipment worked.*

explanation
what something means or why it
happened *There is a good explanation
for the accident.*

▲ How many things can you see
beginning with 'e'?

explode (exploding, exploded)
to suddenly burst or blow up into
small pieces *The fireworks exploded in
the night sky.*

N O P Q R S T U V W X Y Z

explore (exploring, explored)
to look around a new place *We explored the cave.*

explosion
the noise, smoke, and sometimes flames, that are made when something blows up into pieces *The explosion filled the air with smoke.*

extinct
no longer existing
The dodo is an extinct bird.

◀ extinct

extra
more than is necessary *People are nice to you on your birthday.*

eye
the part of the body that animals use to see *What colour are your eyes?*

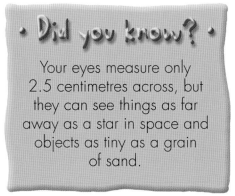

· Did you know? ·

Your eyes measure only 2.5 centimetres across, but they can see things as far away as a star in space and objects as tiny as a grain of sand.

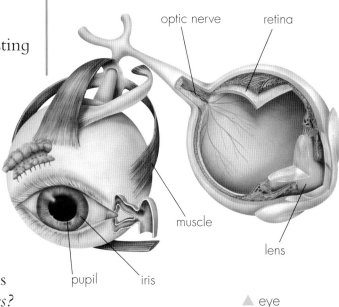

optic nerve   retina

muscle

lens

pupil   iris

▲ eye

A B C D E F G H I J K L M

Ff

face
the front part of your head *She has such a pretty face.*

▶ face

factory
a place where things are made in large numbers by machines and people *Dad works at the car factory.*

faint
1 not strong or easy to hear, see or smell *There is a faint smell of smoke.*
2 feeling weak and light-headed *I am so hungry I feel faint.*

fair
1 good and reasonable *Their decision is fair.*
2 light-coloured *He has fair hair*
3 fine, pleasant *If the weather is fair, we'll go to the beach.*

fairy (fairies)
a magical person with wings *Tinkerbell is the fairy in* Peter Pan.

▶ fairy

fairy tale
a story for children about magical things *Some fairy tales are very old.*

fake
not real *Her coat is fake fur.*

fall (falling, fell, fallen)
to drop downwards *My little brother is learning to walk but he keeps falling over.*

false
not true, correct or real *He gave a false name.*

family (families)
a group of people who are related to each other *There are nine people in their family.*

famous
well-known *He's a famous singer*

fan
1 an object that you hold in your hand and move, or a machine that moves the air to make it cooler *Sit in front of the fan and relax.*
2 someone who likes a particular thing or person very much *My uncle is a Beatles fan.*

far (faraway)
not near, a distance away *I love getting letters from faraway places.*

farm
a place where people grow crops and raise animals *Cows are kept on dairy farms.*

▶ farm

fast
quick, not slow *Racing cars are very fast.*

fat
1 weighing more than is good or normal *It isn't healthy to be too fat.*
2 thick, big or wide *Our teacher reads to us from a big, fat book.*

father
a male parent *Dad reads to me at night.*

favourite
liked the best *Blue is my favourite colour.*

A B C D E F G H I J K L M

fax (faxes)

1 a document sent by fax *There's a fax for you.*
2 a machine that you use to send documents down a telephone line *Use the fax to send a message.*

fear (fearing, feared)

to have the feeling that something bad is going to happen or has happened *There is nothing to fear!*

feast

a large, special meal to celebrate something *Christmas dinner is a feast at our house.*

feather

one of the soft, light things that cover a bird's body *Peacock feathers are beautiful colours.*

▲ feather

feed (feeding, fed)

to give food to a person or an animal *It's fun to feed the chickens.*

◀ feed

feel (feeling, felt)

1 to have an emotion *I feel happy!*
2 to touch or be touched by something *This sweater feels rough.*

female

a woman, girl or animal that can have babies when adult *Female sheep are called ewes.*

fence

a wall made of wood or wire *There are plants growing up our garden fence.*

N O P Q R S T U V W X Y Z

ferry (ferries)

a kind of ship
The ferry leaves at noon.

▶ ferry

few

1 not many *There are few tickets left.*
2 a small number *I have a few friends.*

field

a piece of land for growing crops, raising animals or playing sports *There is a bull in that field.*

fierce

angry and strong, or violent *Guard dogs can be very fierce.*

fight

when two or more people try to hurt each other *I must stop the fight.*

figure

1 a written number *Write all the figures down.*
2 a person's shape *She saw the figure of a woman in the shadows.*

file

1 information on a computer *Move your files to a new folder.*
2 information about a person or subject kept for a reason *The doctor has files on all of the patients.*

fill (filling, filled)

to put things into something until it is full *Fill the vase with water before putting the flowers in.*

film

1 thin plastic that you put into a camera to take photographs *Digital cameras don't use film.*
2 a movie *We saw the film at the cinema.*

A B C D E F G H I J K L M

•Puzzle time•

What's the missing letter?

fin_sh   f_ght
f_eld   f_erce

answer:
finish fight field fierce

find (finding, found)
to see or get something that you are looking for *Can you find the answer?*

fine
1 very thin or in small pieces *The beach is covered with fine, white sand.*
2 very good *They are fine singers.*

finger
one of the five long parts on your hand *Your thumb is a finger.*

finish (finishing, finished)
to end *Put your pencil down when you have finished.*

fire
something that burns, giving out heat and flames *We sat around the fire.*

fire engine
a truck used to put out fires *Fire engines have flashing lights.*

firework
small objects that explode into bright colours in the sky *The fireworks start after dark.*

fish
an animal that lives in water, has fins and breathes through gills *There are seven fish in the tank.*

▶ fish

N O P Q R S T U V W X Y Z

fist
a closed hand *Which fist is the coin in?*

fit
to look and feel healthy *I feel very fit.*

fix (fixing, fixed)
1 to mend, to repair *I can fix the car.*
2 to stick or attach *Fix the picture to the wall.*

flag
a piece of cloth that is used as a signal, or the sign of a country *Stars and stripes are on the flag of the USA.*

▲ flag

flame
burning gas from a fire, or bright light from a candle *The flame is hot!*

flash
a burst of light *The light flashed on.*

flat
1 a room or rooms in a bigger building *My uncle lives in a flat.*
2 not bumpy or hilly, smooth *It's a very flat country.*

flavour
the taste of something *Chocolate and vanilla are flavours of ice cream.*

• Puzzle time •

Can you guess these flavours?

1. v_nilla   2. choc_l_te

3. str_wberr_   4. ban_n_

answers: 1. vanilla 2. chocolate
3. strawberry 4. banana

flight
a journey in a plane *It's a night flight.*

float (floating, floated)
not to sink *Float in the pool.*

A B C D E F G H I J K L M

flood
a lot of water in a place that is usually dry *There were heavy rains and then a flood.*

floor
part of a building that you stand on *Everyone is sitting on the floor.*

petal ▼ flower

stamen

flower
the part of a plant that makes the seeds or fruit *Roses, pansies, and daisies are all flowers.*

stem

fly (flying, flew)
1 to move through the air *We flew at night.*
2 a small insect *A fly buzzed by me.*

fog
mist or cloud *You can't see far in fog.*

fold (folding, folded)
to turn or bend something over on itself *Fold your clothes.*

follow (following, followed)
to move after or behind someone or something *Follow me!*

food
something that people or animals eat *This food tastes delicious.*

foolish
silly *It is a foolish idea.*

foot (feet)
the part of your body at the end of your leg that you stand and walk on *My father has very big feet.*

football
a game that is played by two teams who try to kick a ball into a net to score goals *We play football every day.*

N O P Q R S T U V W X Y Z

forget (forgetting, forgotten)
to not remember something *Don't forget to do your homework.*

fork
1 something with a handle and two or more points that is used for eating *The fork goes to the left of the plate.*
2 a tool used for digging *Turn the soil with a fork.*
3 the place in a road or river that divides in two *The road forks here.*

▲ How many things can you see beginning with 'f'?

forwards
towards the front *Take a step forwards.*

fossil
the print of an animal or plant that lived long ago *Fossils show us what life was like millions of years ago.*

fountain
a jet of water that is pushed up into the air *There is a fountain in the city centre.*

▶ fox

fox (foxes)
a wild animal that looks like a dog with a bushy tail *Baby foxes are called cubs.*

fraction
a part of something *One-half, one-third and one-quarter are fractions.*

frame
the thing that fits around a door, window or picture *Frames can be wood or metal.*

A B C D E F G H I J K L M

freckle
a small, reddish-brown spot on a person's skin *I have freckles on my face.*

free
1 not controlled *Wednesday afternoon is free time at our school.*
2 not costing anything *The Internet is free for schools until 6:30 p.m.*

freeze (freezing, froze, frozen)
to turn to ice because the temperature is very cold *Water freezes at 0°C.*

fresh
1 just picked, grown or made *Fresh fruits and vegetables are healthy foods.*
2 clean and pure *Go and get some fresh air.*

friend
a person you know and like *Good friends are very special.*

friendly
kind and easy to get on with *We have very friendly neighbours.*

frighten (frightening, frightened)
to scare, to make afraid *Storms may frighten animals.*

▶ frog

frog
an animal with long legs that lives on land and in water *There are frogs in the pond.*

· Did you know? ·
Almost any frog can jump 20 times its own length.

front
the part of something that is the most forward *I sit at the front of class.*

N O P Q R S T U V W X Y Z

frost
white, icy powder that forms when it is very cold outside *The trees are covered in frost.*

frown (frowning, frowned)
to have a sad, angry or worried look on your face *Try not to frown.*

fruit
part of a plant that has seeds, such as an apple or grapes *I love fruit!*

▲ fruit

fry (frying, fried)
to cook something using oil *Fry the fish until it is cooked.*

full
containing as much as possible *Is the tank full yet?*

fun
enjoyable *This website is really fun.*

funny
making you laugh *The puppy is very funny.*

▼ fur

fur (furry)
soft, thick hair on the skin of an animal *The kitten has soft, fluffy fur.*

furniture
things such as chairs, tables, beds and desks *We have some new furniture.*

future
the time after now *In the future, we will have computers in our clothes.*

fuzzy
1 not clear *These pictures are fuzzy.*
2 curly and soft *My hair is fuzzy.*

A B C D E F G H I J K L M

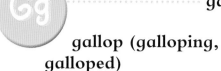

gallop (galloping, galloped)

how animals such as horses or zebras run *The zebras galloped away.*

game

an activity that has rules *Let's play a board game.*

garage

1 a place to keep a car *The garage is next to the house.*
2 a place where cars are repaired *The car is at the garage.*

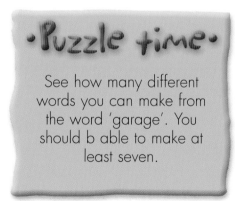

•Puzzle time•

See how many different words you can make from the word 'garage'. You should b able to make at least seven.

garden

land where flowers and plants can be grown *The garden is full of flowers.*

◀ garden

gate

a door in a fence or wall *There is a gate between our garden and our neighbour's.*

gentle

1 kind and careful not to hurt or disturb people or things *She is gentle with the animals.*
2 not loud or strong *There is a gentle breeze blowing.*

N O P Q R S T U V W X Y Z

geography
the study of countries *I like geography because we read about people and places.*

ghost
a dead person's spirit *Do you believe in ghosts?*

giant
an imaginary person who is very big *The story is about a giant.*

▶ giant

gift
something given to someone, a present *That's a lovely gift, thank you.*

giraffe
a very tall wild animal with a long neck *Giraffes live in Africa.*

girl
a female child *There are 15 girls in our class.*

give (gave, given)
1 to let someone have something *We gave our teacher a present.*
2 to pass something to someone *Give this cup to your sister.*

glad
happy about something *We're so glad you could come.*

glass
1 hard, clear material that is used to make windows, bottles and mirrors *The fish live in a glass bowl.*
2 a container for drinking from *I have a glass of water next to my bed.*

•Puzzle time•

Which of these objects is the odd one out ?

glass

bottle

jar

plate

answer: plate

glasses

two pieces of glass or plastic that you wear to protect your eyes or to see better *I wear glasses for reading.*

gloomy

1 dark *It's a gloomy day.*
2 sad *Don't look so gloomy, smile!*

glove

a piece of clothing to wear on your hands *Where are your gloves?*

▼ gloves

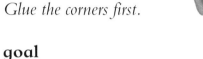

glue (gluing, glued)

to stick things together *Glue the corners first.*

goal

1 the posts in a game such as football or hockey, where the player tries to place the ball *The goalkeeper is a very important player.*
2 the point given to a team when it puts the ball inside the goal *That's another goal for our team.*
3 something you hope to do *My goal is to be a teacher.*

▶ goat

goat

a farm animal that usually has horns *Goats will eat almost anything.*

gold

1 a valuable, yellow metal *The ring is made of gold.*
2 the colour of this metal *The present is wrapped up in gold paper.*

▶ gorilla

good (better, best)

1 of high quality *It's a very good school.*
2 pleasant *I'm having a good time.*
3 well-behaved *They have been really good children.*

goodbye (bye)

something you say when you are leaving someone *Goodbye and good luck!*

goose (geese)

a bird that looks like a big duck *There are geese on the farm.*

goosebumps

little bumps on your skin that appear when you are cold or frightened *The spooky story gave me goosebumps.*

gorilla

the biggest kind of ape *She studies gorillas.*

Did you know? •

Gorillas were relatively unknown animals until the mid 1800s. In fact none were kept in zoos until 1911, in the United States.

grandparents (grandfather, grandmother)

the parents of your mother or father *Our grandparents live with us.*

grape

a small, round, juicy fruit that grows in bunches *Grapes can be red, green or purple.*

▶ grapes

grass

a green plant with thin leaves that grows over the ground *My brother is cutting the grass.*

gravity

the force that pulls things towards Earth and other planets *Gravity is what makes things fall to the ground.*

great

1 very good *This is a great song.*
2 very large *There was a great storm.*

greedy

wanting or taking more than is necessary *He was a greedy king.*

ground

1 the surface of the Earth that is under your feet *Lie on the ground and look up at the stars.*
2 the soil on and under the surface of the Earth *We are digging a hole in the ground near the pond.*
3 land used for a purpose *The football ground is on the edge of town.*

group

people or things that are together or connected *A group of us are playing in the paddling pool.*

▼ group

grow (growing, grew, grown)

to become larger or longer *The flowers are growing very well.*

guard (guarding, guarded)
to protect someone or something
There is a guard outside.

guess (guessing, guessed)
to try to give the right answer when you are not sure if it is correct
Guess which hand it is in.

▶ guinea pig

guinea pig
a furry animal with no tail that people keep as a pet *We have a guinea pig in our classroom.*

▲ How many things can you see beginning with 'g'?

guitar
a stringed musical instrument with a long neck *He plays the guitar in a band.*

◀ guitar

gun
a weapon that fires bullets *Guns are dangerous weapons.*

gym
a place where people go to exercise *There are lots of different machines at the gym.*

A B C D E F **G** **H** I J K L M

Hh

hair
thin threads that grow on your skin and head *She has long, brown hair.*

half (halves)
one of two equal parts *Would you like half an apple?*

ham
meat from a pig's leg *Some ham tastes salty.*

hamburger
minced beef cooked and served in a round bun *I can make hamburgers.*

hammer
a tool used for hitting nails into wood *Use a hammer to bang the nail.*

▶ hammer

▶ hamster

hamster
a small, furry animal like a mouse. *Hamsters keep food in their cheeks.*

hand
the part of your body at the end of your arm *Your fingers and thumb are attached to your hand.*

handbag
a bag used for keeping things in *Mum keeps a hair brush and keys in her handbag.*

handsome
nice-looking *He's a very handsome man.*

N O P Q R S T U V W X Y Z

hang (hanging, hanged, hung)
to attach the top part of something, leaving the lower part free or loose *Sam hung on to the branch.*

happen (happening, happened)
to be, to take place *Who knows what will happen?*

happy
feeling pleased *This is a happy day.*

▲ happy

harbour
a safe place for ships and boats near land *The fishing boats leave the harbour early in the morning.*

hard
1 not soft *This bed is very hard.*
2 difficult, not easy *The questions are very hard.*

hat
a piece of clothing that you wear on your head *You must wear a hat in the sun.*

hate (hating, hated)
to strongly dislike something or someone *Our cat hates going to the vet for her injections.*

head
1 the part of your body above your neck *Put your hands on your head.*
2 a person who is the leader *The head of the school is in charge.*

healthy
well and strong *Our new baby is a healthy girl.*

A B C D E F G H I J K L M

hear (hearing, heard)

1 to be aware of sounds by using your ears *Can you hear the rain?*
2 to get news or be told something *I hear you're moving away.*

heart

1 the part of your body that pumps your blood *Your heart beats faster when you run.*
2 the main part of something *It's in the heart of the city.*
3 a shape that means love *Valentine cards are decorated with hearts.*

heat (heating, heated)

to make something warm *Heat the soup but don't boil it.*

heavy

weighing a lot *These books are heavy.*

hedgehog

a small, wild animal with sharp hairs on its back *Hedgehogs like milk.*

▼ heart

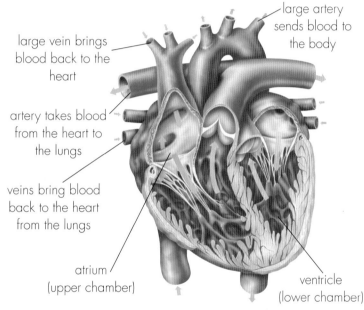

large vein brings blood back to the heart

large artery sends blood to the body

artery takes blood from the heart to the lungs

veins bring blood back to the heart from the lungs

atrium (upper chamber)

ventricle (lower chamber)

heel

1 the back part of your foot *Your heel is under your ankle.*
2 the part of a shoe that is under your heel *Mum's shoes have high heels.*

height

how tall something is *What is your height in centimetres?*

▶ helicopter

helicopter

an aircraft with blades on top that spin and make it fly *Helicopters can land in smaller spaces than planes.*

hello

what you say when you see or meet someone, or when you answer the telephone *Hello! How are you?*

▶ helmet

helmet

a hat that protects your head *Always wear a helmet when you ride your bike.*

help (helping, helped)

to make it easier for someone to do something *Let me help you.*

hen

female chicken *Hens lay eggs.*

here

in this place *I like it here.*

hibernate (hibernating, hibernated)

to sleep during cold weather *Some animals hibernate in winter.*

hide (hiding, hid, hidden)

to put yourself or something out of sight *Hide the presents, she's coming.*

high

1 a long way from the bottom to the top *The mountain is very high.*
2 a long way above *The plane is high above us.*

A B C D E F G H I J K L M

hill
ground that is raised *Run down the hill.*

▶ hill

hippopotamus (hippopotamuses, hippopotami)
a large animal that lives near rivers and lakes in Africa *Hippopotamuses leave the water at night to eat grass.*

history
things that have happened in the past *Our town history is very interesting.*

hit (hitting, hit)
to swing your hand or something you are holding against something else *Hit the ball as hard as you can.*

hobby (hobbies)
something that you enjoy doing in your spare time *My hobbies are skateboarding and listening to music.*

▶ hobby

hockey
a game played by hitting a ball using wooden sticks *Hockey is a very fast game.*

hold (holding, held)
to have something in your hands or arms *Hold my coat, please.*

hole
an opening or an empty space *There's a hole in the bag.*

holiday

1 a special day *It is a religious holiday.*
2 a time when you do not have to work or go to school *School holidays start soon.*

hollow

empty inside *The log is hollow.*

hologram

a picture made with a laser *There is a hologram on the sticker.*

home

the place where you live *What time will you get home?*

homework

school work you do at home *I do my homework when I get home from school.*

honey

a sweet, sticky food made by bees *Put honey in your yoghurt.*

▶ hood

hood

a piece of clothing that covers your head, usually attached to a coat or jacket *Put your hood up, it's raining.*

hoof (hooves)

the foot of an animal, such as a deer, horse or goat *Horses have very thick hooves.*

hook

a piece of metal or plastic for hanging up or catching things *Hang your jacket on the hook.*

A B C D E F G H I J K L M

hoop

a large ring of metal, wood or plastic *It's fun to play with hoops.*

▲ hoops

hop (hopping, hopped)

to jump on one foot, or make a small jump with two feet *Can you hop on one foot?*

hope (hoping, hoped)

to wish for something *I hope you have a good time.*

horn

1 one of the hard, pointed things on an animal's head *Goats have horns.*

2 something that you push to make a noise *The horn is very loud.*

▲ horn

horrible

bad or unpleasant *What a horrible colour.*

horse

a large animal with four legs, a mane and a tail *My brother can ride a horse.*

▶ horse

N O P Q R S T U V W X Y Z

hospital
the place where sick or injured people go to get better *Have you ever stayed in hospital?*

hot
at a very high temperature *Mercury is the hottest planet in the Solar System.*

▲ How many things can you see beginning with 'h'?

hot dog
a sausage in a long bun *Would you like a hot dog?*

hotel
a place people pay to stay in. *There's a hotel on the beach.*

hour
sixty minutes *It will take at least an hour for us to get to work.*

house
a building that people live in *My best friend lives in the house across the street from me.*

huge
very big *There is a huge crowd waiting outside.*

human (human being)
a person, not an animal *Humans are very intelligent.*

hump
a large bump *Some camels have two humps and others have just one.*

hungry
feeling that you need food *I'm hungry. What's for dinner?*

A B C D E F G **H** I J K L M

hunt (hunting, hunted)
1 to look for something or someone *We hunted everywhere for the other shoe.*
2 to try to catch wild animals *The owl hunted for mice at night.*

▶ hunt

hurry (hurrying, hurried)
to do something quickly *Hurry and get your coat.*

hurt (hurting, hurt)
1 to cause pain or harm *The dentist won't hurt you.*
2 to feel pain *My knee hurts.*

husband
the man who a woman is married to *Dad is Mum's husband.*

▼ hurricane

· Did you know? ·

When hunting, owls use sharp claws called talons to grab their prey.

hurricane
a very strong wind storm *Hurricanes can cause lots of damage.*

N O P Q R S T U V W X Y Z

ice

water that is so cold that it has frozen and become hard *Do you want ice in your water?*

◀ ice

iceberg

a large piece of ice that floats in the sea *We saw the tip of an iceberg.*

• **Did you know?** •

Almost 90 percent of an iceberg is below the surface of the water.

ice cream

a frozen, sweet food that is usually made of milk or cream *Ice cream tastes good on hot days.*

ice skate (ice skating, ice skated)

to move across ice wearing boots with a metal blade on the bottom *We're learning how to ice skate.*

▼ icing

icing

a sweet covering for cakes *Spread the icing evenly around the cake.*

idea

a plan or a thought about how to do something *Have you any ideas about how we can raise money for the school outing?*

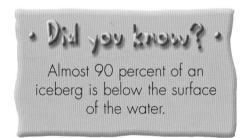
◀ ice cream

A B C D E F G H I J K L M

igloo
an Inuit house made of blocks of snow and ice *Inuit people live in igloos in winter.*

ill
not well, sick *He's feeling quite ill.*

imaginary
not real *The story is about an imaginary cat with special powers.*

imitate (imitating, imitated)
to copy *I can imitate the way you talk.*

immediately
now, at once, right away *Please put your clothes away immediately.*

important
1 serious, useful or valuable *It is a very important discovery.*
2 powerful *The mayor is an important person in our town.*

impossible
not able to be, be done or to happen *That's impossible – you can't be in two places at once!*

information
facts or knowledge about someone or something *There is a lot of information on our website.*

How many things can you see beginning with 'i'?

initial
the first letter of a person's name *What is your middle initial?*

injection
a way of putting medicine into your body using a special needle *The nurse at our school gives injections.*

N O P Q R S T U V W X Y Z

injure (injuring, injured)

to hurt or harm yourself or someone else *Luckily, no one was injured in the crash.*

ink

coloured liquid that is used for writing, drawing or printing *Sign your name in ink.*

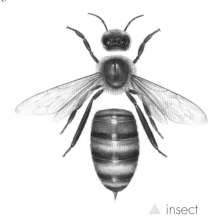

▲ insect

insect

a small animal with six legs, wings and a body that has three parts *Beetles, butterflies and bees are all kinds of insects.*

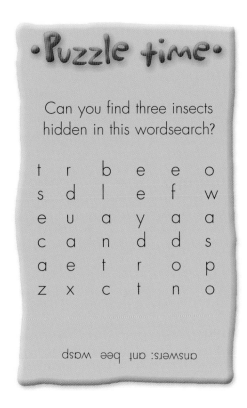

•Puzzle time•

Can you find three insects hidden in this wordsearch?

t r b e e o
s d l e f w
e u a y a a
c a n d d s
a e t r o p
z x c t n o

answers: ant bee wasp

inside

in or into a place or container *Come inside the house, it's very cold out there.*

A B C D E F G H I J K L M

instrument

something people use to do a job
We use instruments to make music.

triangle

tambourine

guitar

drum

▶ instruments

interested

wanting to pay attention to
something or someone so that
you can learn more *Sam is interested
in sport.*

interesting

exciting in a way that keeps your
attention *Emailing children in other
countries is really interesting.*

Internet

a huge system of linked computers
all over the world that lets
people communicate with
each other *We use the
Internet at home and at
school.*

interrupt,
interrupting, interrupted)

to break in or stop someone
who is doing something or
saying something *The phone
call interrupted our conversation.*

invade (invading, invaded)

to attack or go into a place in
large numbers *The Vikings left their
ships and invaded the land.*

invent (inventing, invented)

to make something that has not
been made before *Computers were
invented about 65 years ago.*

invention

something new that someone makes, or produces, for the first time *The telephone is the invention of Alexander Graham Bell.*

telephone (1876)

car (1885)

flying machine (1874)

invisible

not possible to see *You can't read it, it is written in invisible ink!*

invite (inviting, invited)

to ask someone if they would like to do something such as come to a party *Ellie always invites lots of people to her parties.*

invitation

a note or a card that asks you to go to a party *Have you replied to your party invitation?*

iron

1 a strong, hard metal *The machinery is made from iron.*
2 a machine for smoothing clothes *Be careful, the iron gets very hot.*

island

a piece of land that has water all around it *There are thousands of islands in the Pacific Ocean.*

▶ island

A B C D E F G H I J K L M

jacket

a piece of clothing that look like a short coat *You should take a jacket with you.*

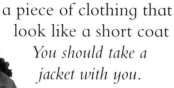

◀ jacket

jail (or gaol)

a prison, a place where people are kept by the police *The thief was put in jail for seven months.*

jam

a sweet food made from fruit *We have toast and jam for breakfast.*

jar

a glass container for storing food *Jam and honey are sold in jars.*

jealous

feeling angry or bad because you want something that someone else has *He is jealous of our grades.*

jeans

trousers made of denim *My favourite clothes are jeans and a t-shirt.*

▶ jeans

jeep

an open vehicle that is used for driving over rough ground *It was a bumpy ride in the jeep.*

jelly

a clear, sweet solid food made from fruit juice *We have ice cream and jelly at birthday parties.*

N O P Q R S T U V W X Y Z

jellyfish

a sea animal that floats on the surface and can sting *There are many different types of jellyfish.*

▲ jellyfish

jet

a fast aeroplane *There are several jet fighters in the air show.*

▲ jets

jewel

a kind of stone that is extremely valuable, such as diamonds, sapphires or rubies *The crown was covered in beautiful jewels.*

jewellery

things such as necklaces, bracelets and earrings that you wear for decoration *She wore jewellery to the party.*

▲ jewellery

jigsaw

a puzzle made from shaped pieces that fit together to make a picture *The jigsaw has 100 pieces.*

▶ jigsaw

job

work that you get paid for doing *She has a new job.*

A B C D E F G H I J K L M

join (joining, joined)
1 to become a member of a club or other group *I've joined the chess club.*
2 to stick or fasten together *Join the two pieces of card.*

joke
a funny story that is told to make people laugh *Do you know any jokes?*

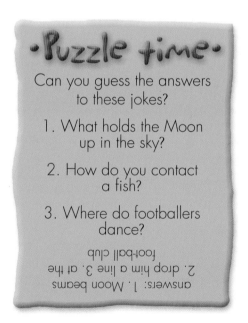

•Puzzle time•

Can you guess the answers to these jokes?

1. What holds the Moon up in the sky?

2. How do you contact a fish?

3. Where do footballers dance?

answers: 1. Moon beams 2. drop him a line 3. at the football club

jolly
happy *He's a jolly person.*

journey
a trip or the distance travelled *We were very tired after the long journey.*

judo
a Japanese fighting sport *In judo, people try to throw each other to the floor.*

jug
a container for liquids *Fill the jug with water.*

▶ juice

juice
liquid from fruit or vegetables *You can have orange juice or apple juice.*

jump (jumping, jumped)

to push yourself off the ground with both feet *Jump as high as you can.*

▲ jump

jumper

a piece of clothing that covers your upper body that you pull over your head *That looks like a nice, warm jumper.*

jungle

a thick forest in a hot country *The trees and plants in a jungle grow very close together.*

▶ jungle

How many things can you see beginning with 'j'?

just

1 to have happened a very short time ago *I've only just arrived home from work.*

2 the right amount or thing *There was just enough flour to make a cake.*

3 only *Don't worry about the new job, it's just a temporary position.*

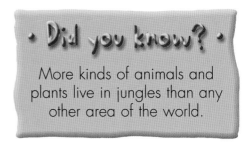

• **Did you know?** •

More kinds of animals and plants live in jungles than any other area of the world.

A B C D E F G H I **J** **K** L M

kaleidoscope

a tube with pictures or pieces of coloured glass or plastic at one end that you look through and turn to see changing patterns *The kaleidoscope was invented in 1816.*

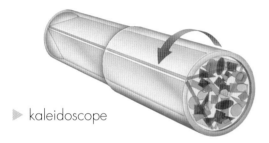

▶ kaleidoscope

kangaroo

an Australian animal that keeps its young in a pouch on the front of its body *Kangaroos have big, strong back legs.*

karate

a Japanese fighting sport *In karate, you fight using your hands and feet.*

▶ karate

keep (keeping, kept)

1 to continue to have something *You can keep the books for two weeks.*
2 to continue to do something *Don't keep staring at that man.*
3 to have something in a certain place *The paints are kept in a cupboard.*

kettle

a container or machine for boiling water *Come in, I'll put the kettle on and make some tea.*

key

1 a piece of metal used to open a lock *Have you seen my front door key?*
2 one of the parts of a computer or piano that you press with your fingers *Type the file name and then press the 'enter' key.*
3 a set of answers or an explanation of symbols *There is a key at the back of the book.*

keyboard

the set of keys on a computer or a piano that you press to type or make a sound *This is a special keyboard with letters and pictures.*

kick (kicking, kicked)

to swing your foot at something *Kick the ball into the goal!*

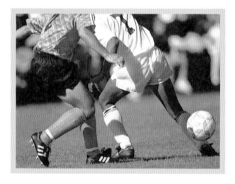

▲ kick

kind

helpful, pleasant and thoughtful *It's very kind of you to think of me.*

king

a royal man who rules a country *Do you think the prince will become king?*

◀ king

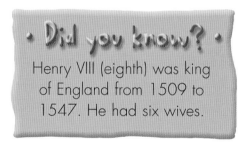

• Did you know? •

Henry VIII (eighth) was king of England from 1509 to 1547. He had six wives.

kill (killing, killed)

to cause someone or something to die *Some weeds kill other plants.*

kiss (kissing, kissed)

to touch someone else with your lips *Mum kissed us all goodnight.*

A B C D E F G H I J K L M

kitchen

the room in a house for preparing food *There are nice smells coming from the kitchen.*

•Puzzle time•

How many kitchen things can you find in this word puzzle?

sinkovencupboardtable
chairshelfcupandsaucer

answer: there are eight things —
sink oven cupboard table chair
shelf cup saucer

kite

a toy made of light wood and cloth, paper or plastic, flown at the end of some string *Shall we fly the kite today?*

kitten

a baby cat *Our cat has had a litter of kittens.*

► kittens

knee

the part of your leg that bends *When you walk, you bend your knees.*

kneel (kneeling, knelt)

to get down on your knees *Dad knelt down to stroke the cat.*

How many things can you see beginning with 'k'?

N O P Q R S T U V W X Y Z

knife

a tool with a blade for cutting things into pieces *Put the knife to the right of your plate.*

knight

a kind of soldier who lived hundreds of years ago *Knights wore armour when they rode into battle.*

knit (knitting, knitted)

to join wool together with long metal sticks *Jodie can knit.*

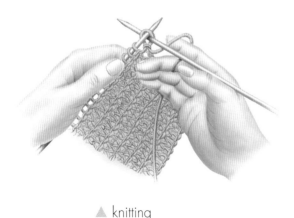

▲ knitting

knock (knocking, knocked)

to hit something to make a noise *Knock on the back door.*

▲ knot

knot

the place where two pieces of string or rope are tied together *There are many different ways that you can tie a knot.*

know

1 to have information or knowledge in your mind *I know that there are nine planets in our Solar System.*
2 to have met someone before or be familiar with them *I know Mrs Smith really well.*

A B C D E F G H I J **K** **L** M

Ll

label

a piece of paper or cloth that gives information about the thing it is attached to *Always put a label on your floppy disks.*

lace

fine cloth made with patterns of tiny holes *The doll's dress is made of lace.*

ladder

a piece of equipment made from two long bars joined together by short bars, which is used for climbing up to reach high places *Dad uses a ladder when he paints the house.*

ladybird

an insect that is red with black spots *Ladybirds are good for the garden.*

▶ ladybird

lake

a big area of water that has land all around it *The lake has frozen.*

▶ lamb

lamb

a young sheep or the meat from that animal *Lambs are born in the spring.*

lamp

a machine that gives light *Switch on the lamp, it's too dark to see.*

land

1 ground *We bought a plot of land.*
2 the dry part of the Earth *The sailors were very happy to see land.*
3 a place or a country *The castle is in a magical land far away.*

land (landing, landed)

to reach the ground after being in the air *The plane lands at 2:45 p.m.*

N O P Q R S T U V W X Y Z

language
words people use to communicate *Our teacher speaks two languages.*

How many things can you see beginning with 'l'?

lap
1 the top of your legs when you are sitting down *My cat sits on my lap.*
2 once around a track *They ran 12 laps of the track.*

large
big *We ate a large piece of cake.*

laser
a powerful light or the machine that makes it *We saw a brilliant laser show at the museum.*

last
1 after the others *We came last in the egg and spoon race.*
2 the one that happened the shortest time ago *We went to Italy for our last holiday.*

last (lasting, lasted)
to continue to work or to be *How long do you think this good weather will last?*

late
1 after the normal or correct time *Sorry I'm late!*
2 towards the end of a period of time *It was late on Sunday afternoon when we left for town.*

laugh (laughing, laughed)
to make a sound that shows you are happy, or when you think something is funny *We laughed at Dad's silly joke.*

law
a rule made by the government
A new law has been passed.

lawn
a place in a garden or a park that is covered in grass that is cut short
Mow the lawn.

lay (laying, laid)
1 to put in a place *Lay the coats over the back of the chair.*
2 to make an egg *The hens lay an egg most days.*

lazy
1 a name given to someone who doesn't like work *She's the laziest girl in the class.*
2 not busy, relaxed *We had a nice, lazy weekend.*

lead (leading, led)
1 to show someone the way *The dog led them to the children.*
2 to be in the front *The champion is leading the parade.*

lean (leaning, leant, leaned)
1 to be in or move into a position that is not straight *Lean over the fence and pick up the ball.*
2 to rest against something *Chris was leaning against the wall, watching the match.*

leap (leaping, leapt)
to jump into the air or over something *The frog leapt into the pond.*

◀ leap

learn (learning, learnt, learned)
to get knowledge or information about a subject *We are learning to paint pictures at school.*

leave (leaving, left)
1 to go away from a place *What time are you leaving?*
2 to put a thing in a place or to let a thing stay in a place *You can leave your bike in the garden.*

leg
1 the part of your body that you stand up with, between your hip and your foot *Dad's legs are a lot longer than mine are.*
2 the part of a table or chair that holds it up *One of the chair legs is broken.*

lemon
a sour yellow fruit *We put lemon juice and sugar on the pancakes.*

lend (lending, lent)
to let someone have or use something that they will return after using *Lend me a pen, please.*

leopard
a large cat with yellow or white fur and black spots *Leopards are beautiful animals.*

◀ leopard

leotard
a stretchy piece of clothing that you wear for dancing or exercising *We wear leotards in ballet class.*

lesson
a time in which someone is taught something such as a skill or a subject *I go to extra French lessons every Thursday after school.*

let (letting, let)
1 to allow someone to do something *Will your mum let you sleep over tonight?*
2 to allow something to happen *Just let the ball fall.*

letter
1 one of the signs of the alphabet used in writing *There are five letters in James' name.*
2 a written message that you put in an envelope and send or give someone *You can either send a letter or an email.*

lettuce
a green, leafy vegetable eaten in salads *We're growing lettuce this year.*

▶ lettuce

library
a place where books are kept *A mobile library comes to our village twice a week.*

lick (licking, licked)
to put your tongue on something *Lick your ice cream, it's going to drip.*

lie (lying, lay, lain)
to have your body flat on the floor, ground or bed. *We put our towels on the sand and lay down.*

lie (lying, lied)
to say something that is not the truth *They lied about their age.*

life (lives)
1 the time between when you are born and when you die *He had a long, happy life.*
2 being alive *Do you think there is life on other planets?*

N O P Q R S T U V W X Y Z

lifeboat
a boat that helps people who are in danger at sea *The fishermen were rescued by the lifeboat just in time.*

lift
1 a machine that takes you up and down in a building *Take the lift to the fourth floor.*
2 a ride in a car *Do you need a lift?*

lift (lifting, lifted)
to move something to a higher place *It took four people to lift our piano.*

light
1 energy or brightness from the Sun or a lamp that lets you see things *Is there enough light to take a picture?*
2 a machine that makes light *Turn off the light, it's time for bed.*

lighthouse
a tower on the coast that has a bright light that flashes to warn ships *There's a lighthouse at the end of the beach.*

lightning
electrical light in the sky during a storm *We could see lightning in the distance.*

like (liking, liked)
1 to enjoy something or be fond of someone or something *I really like skateboarding.*
2 to want *What would you like for your birthday?*

prism

▶ light

light splits into the seven colours of the rainbow when it passes through a prism (glass triangle)

A B C D E F G H I J K L M

line
1 a long, thin mark *Draw a line through the mistakes.*
2 a piece of string, rope or wire *Hang the clothes on the line.*
3 a row *There is a line of trees as you go into the park.*

▶ lion

lion
a large wild cat *Lions live in Africa.*

lips
the edges of your mouth *The cat came in, licking his lips.*

liquid
something, such as water, that is not hard and can be poured *There's some liquid soap in the bathroom.*

listen (listening, listened)
to pay attention to sound *Sorry, what did you say? I wasn't listening.*

litter
1 rubbish lying on the ground *We picked up all the litter in the playground.*
2 the group of babies that an animal has at one time *Our dog had a litter of puppies last night.*

little
small, not large or not much *We gave the cat a little milk.*

live (living, lived)
1 to be alive *My great grandfather lived to be 80 years old.*
2 to have your home in a certain place *They live in France now.*

living room
a room in a house for sitting and relaxing in *The TV is in the living room.*

N O P Q R S T U V W X Y Z

lizard
a short, four-legged animal that lays eggs *Lizards are cold-blooded animals.*

loaf (loaves)
bread that is baked in one piece *Get a loaf of bread and some milk from the shop.*

◀ lizard

lobster
a sea animal with eight legs and two claws *We saw a lobster through the glass bottom of the boat.*

▼ lobster

lock
an object that is used to close something, usually opened and shut with a key *There's a lock on the chest.*

lock (locking, locked)
to close or fasten something with a key *Have you locked the door?*

loft
the inside of the roof of a house *There's an old tennis racket in the loft.*

log
a thick piece of a tree *It's cold in here, put another log on the fire.*

lonely
feeling sad that you are on your own *Come over if you get lonely.*

long
1 measuring a big distance from one end to the other *Is it a long walk?*
2 continuing for a large amount of time *It's a very long movie.*

look (looking, looked)
to pay attention to something that you see *Look at that hot air balloon.*

A B C D E F G H I J K **L** M

loose
1 not tight *Wear loose clothes.*
2 free to move *The lions were set loose.*

lose (losing, lost)
1 to not be able to find something *He keeps losing his glasses.*
2 to not win a competition or a game *Our team lost the competition.*

loud
not quiet, making a lot of noise *Turn the music down, that's too loud!*

love (loving, loved)
to like someone or something very much *We love our new baby.*

lovely
beautiful or pleasant *It's a lovely day.*

low
close to the ground, not high *There are some low clouds around the hills.*

lucky
1 fortunate, having good things happen to you *They're lucky they won.*
2 giving good luck *These are my lucky football boots.*

lunch
a meal that you eat in the middle of the day *Why don't we meet for lunch?*

▲ lunch

lungs
parts of your body inside your chest that help you to breathe *You have two lungs protected by bones called ribs.*

N O P Q R S T U V W X Y Z

machine

a piece of equipment that is used to do a job *Washing machines wash, rinse and spin your clothes.*

◀ machine

magic

a power to make strange things happen *I can do magic tricks.*

magnet

a piece of metal that makes some other metal objects move towards it *Use a magnet to pick up all the pins.*

main

the most important or the biggest *We'll meet you in front of the main entrance.*

make (making, made)

1 to create or build something *The computer was made in a factory.*
2 to cause something to happen or be a certain way *That joke always makes me laugh.*

male

a man, boy or an animal that cannot produce eggs or have babies *Male elephants are bigger than female elephants.*

mammal

the group of animals that give birth to live babies and make milk for them to drink *The elephant is the largest land mammal.*

◀ mammal

A B C D E F G H I J K L M

man (men)
an adult male *That is a men's shop.*

many
large in number *There are many good reasons to use the Internet.*

map
a drawing that shows where things are in a building, town, country or other place *We studied a map of the world.*

▶ marbles

marble
1 a type of hard stone *The walls are marble.*
2 a small glass or metal ball used to play a game *I won two marbles in that last game.*

march (marching, marched)
to walk with regular steps *The band marched at the front of the parade.*

mark
1 a sign or shape *Put a mark to show where your house is.*
2 a letter or number that a teacher puts on a piece of work to show how good it is *She's getting really good marks this term.*
3 a spot or a dark patch on something that makes it look bad *There is a mark on the carpet where we spilled the juice.*

market
a place where you can buy food, clothes, plants and other things *Most markets are outdoors.*

marmalade
jam that is made from oranges *We had toast and marmalade for breakfast.*

N O P Q R S T U V W X Y Z

marry (marrying, married)
to become husband and wife *They married three years ago.*

mask
something that you put over your face to hide or protect it *He always wore a mask.*

◀ mask

mat
a piece of material that covers a floor or table *Wipe your feet on the mat.*

match (matches)
1 a small stick that makes a flame when you rub it against something *We have special long matches for lighting the fire.*
2 a contest or game *That's the best football match I've ever seen.*

mathematics (maths)
the study of numbers or shapes *Mathematics is studied in schools.*

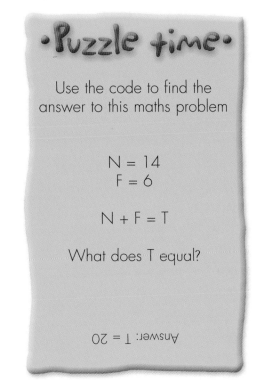

•Puzzle time•

Use the code to find the answer to this maths problem

N = 14
F = 6

N + F = T

What does T equal?

Answer: T = 20

meadow
a field with grass and flowers *The meadow was covered in pretty flowers.*

meal
a time when food is eaten or the actual food itself *Sometimes you feel sleepy after a big meal.*

mean
1 cruel or unkind *Don't be mean to each other.*
2 someone who does not want to spend money *The king is very mean – maybe that's why he's so rich.*

meaning
the information that is supposed to be understood from the use of words and signs *Can you explain the meaning of this sentence?*

measles
an illness that that can give you a high temperature and lots of red spots *When my little brother had measles, he had to stay in bed.*

measure (measures, measuring, measured)
to find out the size or amount of something *Measure each side of the room.*

meat
food made from animals *people who don't eat meat are called vegetarians.*

mechanic
a person who fixes cars and machines *He's a good mechanic.*

medal
a piece of metal that is given as a prize for winning a competition or for doing something special *He won a medal for bravery.*

◀ medal

N O P Q R S T U V W X Y Z

medicine
1 something that you take when you are not well so that you will get better *You have to take this medicine three times a day.*
2 the study of illness and injury *She is studying medicine.*

medium
a middle size between large and small *I'd like a medium popcorn, please.*

meet (meeting, met)
1 to know someone for the first time *We met the first day of school.*
2 to go to the same place as another person *Where shall we meet?*

melody (melodies)
a song or the tune of a song *The song has a strange but beautiful melody.*

melon
a fruit with a hard skin and flat seeds *Melons can be green, yellow or orange.*

melt (melting, melted)
to change from a solid to a liquid when heated *The ice in my drink has melted.*

◀ melt

memory (memories)
1 something that you remember from the past *Photographs bring back memories.*
2 the ability to remember things *Do you have a good memory?*
3 the part of a computer where information is stored *This computer has more memory than our old one.*

mend (mending, mended)
to repair *Could you help me mend the tyre?*

A B C D E F G H I J K L M

menu

1 the list of food in a café or restaurant *The waiter brought us each a menu.*

2 a list of things seen on a computer screen *Click here to go back to the main menu.*

message

information for a person from someone else *Leave a message for him on the note pad.*

messy

not tidy *This room is very messy.*

▲ How many things can you see beginning with 'm'?

metal

hard material such as gold, silver, copper or iron *Silver is a metal.*

microphone

something that is used for recording sounds or making them louder *Speak into the microphone.*

· Did you know? ·
The microphone was developed by Alexander Graham Bell in 1876.

microscope

something that makes small things look much bigger *We looked at a hair under the microscope.*

microwave

an oven that cooks food very quickly using waves of electricity *Heat the soup in the microwave.*

N O P Q R S T U V W X Y Z

midday
12:00 in the middle of the day *We'll have our lunch early – at about midday.*

middle
the centre or the part of something that is between the beginning and the end *We sat down in the middle of the row.*

midnight
12:00 in the middle of the night *We stay up until midnight on New Year's Eve.*

▼ mirror

mild
1 not too strong or serious *She had a mild case of flu.*
2 not tasting too strong or too spicy *It's a mild curry.*
3 not too cold *The weather is mild today.*

milk
white liquid that female humans and other mammals produce to feed their babies *Milk is good for you.*

▷ milk

minus (minuses)
1 the sign used in maths when taking one number away from another *Twenty-five minus five equals twenty.*
2 in temperature, below zero *It's cold today, it's below minus one outside!*

minute
sixty seconds *We waited for twenty minutes but they didn't come.*

mirror
special glass that you can see your reflection or what's behind you in *Go and look in the mirror – you look really funny.*

A B C D E F G H I J K L **M**

miserable
very unhappy *Don't look so miserable.*

miss
not to hit a target *He missed the basket.*

mistake
something that is wrong *We all make mistakes.*

▶ mittens

mittens
gloves that do not have separate places for each finger *Wrap up well and wear your mittens.*

mix (mixing, mixed)
to put different things together *Mix the eggs and flour together.*

mobile phone
a small telephone that people can carry around *Call me on the mobile phone.*

model
1 a small copy of something such as a plane or a building *We made a model plane at the weekend.*
2 a person whose job is to show clothes *She wants to be a model.*
3 one type of something *This computer is the most up-to-date model.*

money
coins and paper that you use to buy things with *Have you spent all your money already?*

monitor
the part of a computer that shows the screen *It's easier to see on a big monitor.*

▼ monkey

monkey
an animal with a long tail that uses its legs to climb *We watched the monkeys at the zoo.*

N O P Q R S T U V W X Y Z

monster

a frightening creature in stories and films *The monster chased them into the forest.*

month

one of the twelve parts of the year *Months are 30 or 31 days long, except February.*

Moon

the small planet that travels around the Earth *The Moon is full tonight.*

more (most)

1 stronger or greater than *This book is more interesting.*
2 a larger or an additional amount or number *Is there any more cake?*

morning

the part of the day between the time the sun comes up and noon *We get up at the same time every morning.*

mosque

a building where Muslim people go to pray *The mosque is in the centre of the town.*

Puzzle time

Spot five differences between these two pictures

A B C D E F G H I J K L **M**

moth
an insect that is similar to a butterfly
Moths are more active at night.

mother
a woman who has a child or a
female animal that has young *My
mother is a nurse.*

motor
the part of a machine that uses
power to make it work *There is a
motor in the washing machine.*

motorbike (motorcycle)
a vehicle with two
wheels and a seat for
people to ride on *Dad
has a new motorbike.*

▶ motorbike

mountain
land that has been pushed
up very high *Some mountains have
snow on top all year round.*

mouse (mice)
1 a small animal with a long tail
and a pointed nose *There are mice in
the field.*
2 the part of a computer with a
ball in it that you move by hand
to move things around
on the screen
*You can play
this game
using a mouse.*

▲ mouse

moustache
the hair that grows above a man's
lip *He has a little moustache.*

mouth
the part of your face that you use
to talk and eat *Don't talk with
your mouth full.*

move (moving, moved)
to change the position of something
Could you move, I can't see the TV?

N O P Q R S T U V W X Y Z

movie
a story that is told using pictures that move, a film *What movie would you like to see tonight?*

much
a lot *Thank you so much for coming.*

mud
wet soil or earth *I'm covered in mud!*

mug
a cup with tall sides *Do you want a mug of hot chocolate?*

multiply (multiplies, multiplying)
to add a number to itself, often more than once *two multiplied by two is four.*

munch (munches, munching, munched)
to eat something noisily *The rabbit munched on carrots and lettuce.*

muscle
one of the parts of the body that tightens and relaxes to cause movement *Relax your muscles.*

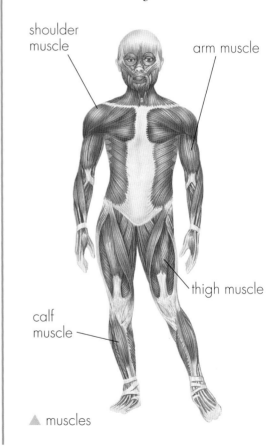

shoulder muscle

arm muscle

thigh muscle

calf muscle

▲ muscles

A B C D E F G H I J K L M

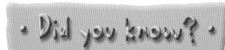

• Did you know? •

The human body has about 620 muscles. You use 200 muscles with every step you take and the tiny muscles in your eye are used up to 100,000 times every day!

music

a pattern of sounds that is sung or played on special instruments *Can you read music?*

▶ music

museum

a place where old, important, valuable or interesting things are kept so that people can go and look at them *There is a toy museum in our town.*

must

to have to do something *You must lock the door before going to bed at night.*

mysterious

something strange, secret or difficult to understand *He is a mysterious person, we don't know much about him.*

mushroom

a small vegetable that has a stem with a round top *Do you want mushrooms on your pizza?*

▶ mushrooms

N O P Q R S T U V W X Y Z

Nn

nail

1 a thin, sharp piece of metal with one flat end that you hit with a hammer *Hang the picture on that nail.*
2 the hard covering on the ends of your fingers and toes *He bites his nails.*

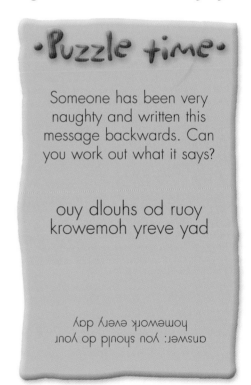

▲ nails

name

what a person or object is called *What's your name?*

narrow

having only a short distance from one side to the other *The road is very narrow.*

nasty

very unpleasant or bad *That's a very nasty cut.*

nation

a country and the people who live there *It is a poor nation.*

naughty

badly behaved *Don't be naughty.*

•Puzzle time•

Someone has been very naughty and written this message backwards. Can you work out what it says?

ouy dlouhs od ruoy krowemoh yreve yad

answer: you should do your homework every day

A B C D E F G H I J K L M

navy

the ships and people that fight for a country at sea during a war *My cousin is in the navy.*

near

close by, not far *There's a bus stop near the zoo.*

neat

1 clean or organised *His room is always neat and tidy.*
2 clearly presented *You have very neat handwriting.*

neck

the part of your body that attaches your head to your shoulders *Put a scarf around your neck.*

necklace

a piece of jewellery that you wear around your neck *That's a beautiful necklace.*

needle

1 a thin, sharp piece of metal with a hole through it used for sewing *First, thread the needle.*
2 a thin, sharp piece of metal through which injections are given *The needle will not hurt you.*

neighbour

a person who lives near another person *We invited all our friends and neighbours to the party.*

nephew

the son of your sister or brother *My nephew is staying with us for a few days.*

▶ necklace

N O P Q R S T U V W X Y Z

nervous

worried or frightened, not able to relax *She's a little nervous about being in the school play.*

▲ nest

nest

a place birds make to lay their eggs *There's a robin's nest in that tree.*

• Did you know? •

The weaver bird 'weaves' a complicated nest out of twigs and dry grass.

net

material that is made by joining pieces of string or thread together, leaving spaces between them *We use a small net when we go fishing.*

▲ net

network

a system of things or people that are connected *Link to a computer network.*

A B C D E F G H I J K L M

never

not at any time, not ever *I've never been to China.*

new

not old or used *I love your jacket, is it new?*

news

information about something that is happening now or that happened a short time ago *Write soon and send us all your news.*

newspaper

sheets of paper that are printed with words and pictures to tell you what is happening in the world *Have you read today's newspaper?*

next

the one that is nearest or immediately after another one *Who's next on the list?*

nice

enjoyable, good, pleasant *Did you have a nice time?*

niece

the daughter of your sister or brother *Her niece works in a bank.*

▲ night

night

the time of day between when the sun sets and rises again *The moon can be seen at night.*

nightgown (nightie)

a dress to sleep in *Put your nightgown on and get into bed.*

N O P Q R S T U V W X Y Z

nightmare
a bad dream *Nightmares can be very scary.*

nobody
no one, no person *There's nobody home.*

nod (nodding, nodded)
to quickly move your head up and down *She nodded her head in agreement with him.*

noise
loud sounds *Please keep the noise down, will you?*

noisy
very loud *There was noisy music coming from the concert hall.*

none
not any, not one *Sorry, there is none left in the box.*

nonsense
something that does not make any sense, or mean anything *The television programme was complete nonsense.*

noodles
very thin strips of food that are usually made from flour, water and eggs and then boiled *Do you want rice or noodles?*

▼ noodles

noon
midday, 12:00 *Shall we meet at noon tomorrow for lunch?*

A B C D E F G H I J K L M

no one

nobody, not one person *I have no one to talk to.*

normal

something that is ordinary or usual *It's normal to feel tired first thing in the morning.*

▼ nose

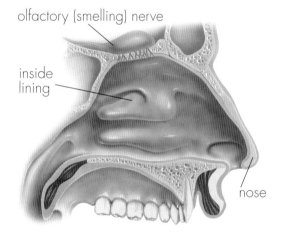

olfactory (smelling) nerve

inside lining

nose

nose

the part of your face that you use for breathing and smelling things *Breathe in deeply through your nose.*

note

1 a short written message *Mum wrote a note to the school.*
2 a piece of paper money *We paid with notes and coins.*
3 a musical sound or the mark to show a musical sound *The opera singer can hit very high notes.*

▶ note

N O P Q R S T U V W X Y Z

nothing

not anything, zero *There's nothing in the box, it's empty.*

notice (noticing, noticed)

1 to see something, or be aware that it is there *Did you notice if anyone was in the shop?*
2 a sign that tells people something *The notice says that the play starts tomorrow.*

novel

a long story in a book, which is written by an author *Have you read his latest novel?*

now

this time, the present *Where are you going now?*

nowhere

not anywhere *Your PE kit is nowhere to be found.*

number

1 a word or symbol that means the amount, quantity or order of something *Some people think seven is a lucky number.*
2 the numbers you press on a phone to call someone *What's your new number?*

▼ nurse

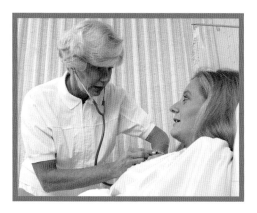

nurse

a person whose job is to take care of people who are sick or hurt *Go and see the school nurse, you don't look well.*

A B C D E F G H I J K L M

nursery (nurseries)

1 a place where small children are looked after during the day while their parents are at work *My little brother still goes to nursery.*

2 a place where plants are grown and sold *We bought some beautiful plants at the nursery on the hill.*

nursery rhyme

a poem or song usually written for young children *My favourite nursery rhymes are 'Jack and Jill', 'Baa Baa Black Sheep' and 'Humpty Dumpty'.*

▲ How many things can you see beginning with 'n'?

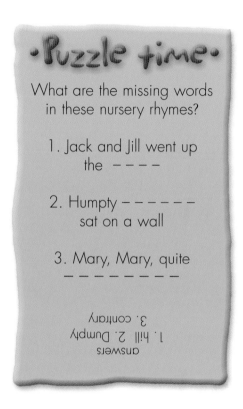

•Puzzle time•

What are the missing words in these nursery rhymes?

1. Jack and Jill went up the – – – –

2. Humpty – – – – – – sat on a wall

3. Mary, Mary, quite – – – – – – – –

answers
1. hill 2. Dumpty 3. contrary

nut

a seed that you can eat *Peanuts, cashews and almonds are all different types of nuts.*

Oo

ocean

1 the salt water that covers most of the Earth *Strange fish live at the bottom of the ocean.*
2 a large sea *The Pacific Ocean is the largest ocean.*

· Did you know? ·

About 97 percent of all the water on Earth is in the oceans. The Pacific is the biggest and is twice as big as the next largest ocean, the Atlantic. This is followed by the Indian, Southern and Arctic Oceans.

octopus

a sea animal that has eight legs *The legs of the octopus are called tentacles.*

off

1 not on *Take the glass off the table.*
2 not in use or switched on *Shut the computer down before you switch it off.*
3 away from *Keep off the grass.*

office

a place where people work at desks *There are four people in my Mum's office.*

oil

1 a thick liquid made from plants or animals and used for cooking *Put a little olive oil in the pan.*
2 a thick liquid that comes out of the ground and is used to make petrol *They discovered oil there last year.*
3 a thick liquid that is used on metal or wood so that parts move better or more easily *This door is squeaking. Can you put some oil on it, please?*

◀ octopus

A B C D E F G H I J K L M

okay (OK)
1 fine, healthy, well *Are you okay?*
2 all right *Is it okay if I copy my work to your computer?*

old
not young, not new *My grandad is getting very old.*

◀ old

once
1 one time *We've met only once.*
2 one time in a fixed period *We go swimming once a week.*

▼ onions

onion
a vegetable that has a strong smell and taste *Do you want onion on your pizza?*

open
not closed or covered over *What time does the shop open?*

operation
when a doctor cuts open a person's body to mend or remove something *The operation took two hours.*

opposite
1 completely different *The opposite of near is far.*
2 across from, facing *They live in the house opposite.*

▶ orange

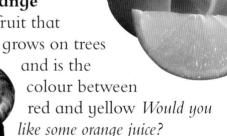

orange
a fruit that grows on trees and is the colour between red and yellow *Would you like some orange juice?*

N O P Q R S T U V W X Y Z

orbit (orbiting, orbited)
to travel round and round something, like a planet in space *The Earth orbits the Sun.*

orchestra
a group of people playing musical instruments together *He plays violin with the school orchestra.*

▲ How many things can you see beginning with 'o'?

•Puzzle time•

Can you name all these orchestral instruments?

1.

2.

3.

4.

answers
1. flute 2. drum 3. violin 4. cello

order
1 to ask for something in a restaurant, shop or on the Internet *Can I order a coffee, please?*
2 to tell someone what to do *The captain ordered the men to attack the ship.*

ordinary
not special, normal *It's just an ordinary house.*

ostrich
a large, African bird with a long neck *Ostriches cannot fly.*

A B C D E F G H I J K L M

otter
a brown, furry wild animal that swims and eats fish *Otters are rarely seen.*

▼ otter

out
1 not in *The mouse got out of his cage.*
2 not at home *She's out at the moment.*
3 out of – none left *We're out of sugar.*

outdoors
not inside a building, in the open air *It's much cooler outdoors.*

oven
something that you use to bake or roast food *Bake the cake in the oven for 45 minutes.*

over
1 above, covering *He put a blanket over us.*
2 finished, ended *Is the film over yet?*
3 from one side to another *A bridge runs over the river.*

owl
a bird that hunts at night *Sometimes you can hear an owl hooting.*

own (owning, owned)
to have something that you bought or were given *We own a new house.*

oxygen
a gas that animals and plants need to live *There is an oxygen mask above your seat.*

Pp

pack (packing, packed)
to put things into boxes, bags or suitcases *Don't forget to pack your suitcases.*

▶ pack

package
a small parcel *This package has your name on it.*

paddle (paddling, paddled)
1 to move a boat through water using oars or your hands *They paddled the canoe across the lake.*
2 to walk in shallow water *My little brother can't swim yet, but he likes to paddle.*

page
one side of a sheet of paper in a book, magazine or newspaper *This book has 128 pages.*

pain
the feeling you have when you are hurt or ill *I have a bad pain in my side.*

paint
a sticky liquid that you brush onto things to colour them *Don't spill paint on the carpet.*

▲ paint

pair
1 two things that go together *I need a new pair of trainers.*
2 something that is made of two similar things joined together *I've bought a new pair of sunglasses for my holiday.*

A B C D E F G H I J K L M

palace
a large, especially fine house where a king, queen or other important person lives *The palace is surrounded by beautiful gardens.*

·Puzzle time·

Can you find all the pairs in this picture?

answer: jeans socks gloves scissors trainers

palm
1 the inside part of your hand *Fortune tellers read palms.*
2 a kind of tree with leaves only at the top *Our tent was under a row of palms on the beach.*

pan
a round cooking pot with a long handle *Melt the butter in a pan.*

pancake
a thin, flat cake that is cooked in a frying pan *I like pancakes with sugar.*

panda
a large, black and white animal that looks like a bear *Pandas come from China.*

pantomime
a funny musical show for children that is performed around Christmas *The pantomime is 'Robin Hood'.*

N O **P** Q R S T U V W X Y Z

paper
1 thin sheets of material for writing or printing on *There is no paper in the printer.*
2 a newspaper *We recycle our newspapers once a week.*

parachute
a piece of equipment made of cloth that people wear to let them fall slowly through the air *The parachute will open automatically.*

parade
a number of people walking or marching in a long line to celebrate a special occasion *There is a parade every year.*

◀ parade

parent
a mother or father *We're making a special dinner for our parents.*

park
a piece of ground with trees and grass *Let's go to the park to play.*

park (parking, parked)
to put a car, truck, bus or bike in a place for a time *You can park right in front of the library.*

parrot
a tropical bird with coloured feathers *My parrot can say my name.*

part
1 one of the pieces or sections that something is divided into *Would you like part of my orange?*
2 the role of an actor in a film or a play *Who is playing the part of the princess?*

A B C D E F G H I J K L M

party (parties)
a group of people gathered together to enjoy themselves *The party is on Saturday.*

▼ party

pass (passing, passed)
1 to go beyond or past a person, place or thing *You'll pass the bakery on your way.*
2 to succeed in doing something such as a test or an examination *I hope you pass your driving test.*
3 to give someone something *Please pass the strawberries.*

passenger
someone who travels in a vehicle that is controlled by someone else *This plane has seats for 48 passengers.*

Passover
a Jewish holiday held in the spring. *All of the family get together for Passover.*

past
1 after *Let's meet at half past six.*
2 up to and beyond *The bank is on this street, just past the supermarket.*
3 the time before the present *In the past, there was no such thing as email.*

pasta
food made from flour, eggs and water, cut into shapes *Pasta is tasty.*

▶ pasta

paste
1 a type of glue that is used for sticking paper *You can make paste with flour and water.*
2 a soft, spreadable mixture *He likes fish paste sandwiches.*

patch (patches)
1 material to cover a hole in something *I put a patch on my jeans.*
2 a small piece of land *We have a vegetable patch this summer.*

•Puzzle time•

What grows in a vegetable patch? Unscramble these words to find out!

1. tscrrao   2. bbcaaseg
3. ttoomaes   4. snaeb

answers: 1. carrots 2. cabbages
3. tomatoes 4. beans

pattern
1 lines, shapes or colours arranged in a certain way *The pattern that is on the cushions matches the pattern on the curtains.*
2 a shape that you copy or use as a guide to make something *Mum used a pattern to make this jacket for me.*

pavement
the path you walk on next to a road *The cycle path runs between the pavement and the road.*

paw
the foot of an animal *Our dog has a sore paw.*

pay (paying, paid)
to give someone money for something that you are buying, or because someone has done work for you *Don't worry, I'll pay for the theatre tickets.*

A B C D E F G H I J K L M

pea

a small, round green seed that is eaten as food *Would you like peas with your dinner?*

▶ peas

peace

1 no war or fighting *There has been peace between them for many years.*
2 quiet, calmness *She shut the door for a little peace and quiet.*

peach (peaches)

a soft fruit with a large seed inside it *This is a sweet, juicy peach.*

peacock

a male bird with long, brightly coloured tail feathers that spread out like a fan *Peacocks usually have green and blue feathers.*

peanut

a small nut with a soft, bumpy shell *Those peanuts taste very salty.*

pedal

1 part of a bicycle that you push with your feet to make the wheels go round *Can you reach the pedals?*
2 part of a car that you push with your feet to make it stop and go *The brake pedal is for stopping the car.*

peel (peeling, peeled)

to take the skin off a fruit or a vegetable *I helped peel the potatoes.*

pen

an object for drawing and writing with ink *Sign this with a black pen.*

▶ pencils

pencil

an object used for drawing and writing that has lead, not ink, in it *Do the crossword with a pencil.*

penguin

a black and white sea bird that cannot fly *Penguins use their wings to help them swim.*

• Did you know? •

Penguins usually have one or two eggs at a time. Both parents take turns keeping the eggs warm. Later, the young are looked after in a group, usually by the males.

▲ penguins

penny (pence)

one pence *These sweets are a penny each.*

pepper

1 a hot powder used to flavour food *Please pass the salt and pepper.*
2 a sweet or hot-tasting vegetable *Peppers may be green, red, yellow or orange.*

perfume

a liquid with a pleasant smell that you put on your skin *What perfume are you wearing?*

person (people, persons)

a human being, a man, woman or child *Our geography teacher is a very interesting person.*

pet

an animal that is kept at someone's home *Do you have any pets?*

petrol

liquid fuel that makes a car engine run *We need to stop for petrol.*

A B C D E F G H I J K L M

phone (phoning, phoned)
to call someone on the telephone *Joe phoned while you were out.*

photo (photograph)
a picture made with a camera *We had our photos taken for our passports.*

piano
a musical instrument *I play the piano.*

▲ How many things can you see beginning with 'p'?

pick (picking, picked)
1 to choose *I was picked for the team.*
2 to break off a flower or a piece of fruit from a plant *I picked an apple.*
3 to pull pieces off or out of something *Pick the meat from the bone.*

picnic
food that you take outdoors to eat *We had a picnic in the park.*

picture
a drawing, painting or photograph *The winner's picture will be in the paper.*

pie
food made with fruit, vegetables, fish or meat that is baked inside pastry *Would you like another piece of pie?*

▶ pies

piece
a part of something that has been separated or broken *Careful, there are some pieces of glass on the floor.*

pig
an animal with pink skin and a curly tail *A baby pig is called a piglet.*

pile

a lot of things put on top of each other *There's a pile of clothes on the floor.*

▶ pineapple

pillow

a cushion to put your head on in bed *I put my tooth underneath my pillow.*

pilot

the person who is in control of a plane *The pilot showed us the plane's control panel.*

pin

a sharp, thin piece of metal that is used to fasten things or hold pieces of cloth together *Take all the pins out before you try that on.*

pineapple

a brown fruit that is yellow inside and has pointed leaves that stick out of the top *Pineapple juice is my favourite drink.*

pirate

a person who goes onto boats and ships to steal the things they are carrying *The ship was attacked by a group of pirates.*

pizza

a thin, flat round bread that is covered with tomatoes, cheese and other toppings then baked in an oven *We're going to have pizza at the party.*

place

where something is, the position, point or other location *What's the name of the place where we went on holiday last year?*

A B C D E F G H I J K L M

plain

1 one colour, having no pattern or decoration *The curtains are plain green.*
2 easy to understand *Can you tell me in plain English?*
3 not fancy or complicated *It's a plain room, but very clean and neat.*

plan

1 an idea about what will happen in the future *We have holiday plans.*
2 a drawing of a room, building or other space *We drew a plan of our playground.*

plane

an aeroplane *The plane took off from the airport on time.*

planet

one of the very large, round objects that moves around the Sun *There are nine planets in our Solar System.*

▼ planets

Jupiter
Uranus
Pluto
Mars
Neptune
Mercury
Venus
Saturn
Earth

plan (planning, planned)

to think about what you want to do and how to do it *Let's plan a party.*

plant

a living thing that has roots, leaves and seeds and can make its own food *Water the plants every day.*

N O P Q R S T U V W X Y Z

plant (planting, planted)
to put seeds or plants into the ground or containers so they will grow *Plant the seeds in early summer.*

plaster
1 a thick paste that hardens when it dries *Plaster is used to cover walls.*
2 a thin piece of plastic or cloth that you put over a cut or sore *I have a plaster on my knee.*

plastic
a light material that is made from chemicals *The bucket is made of plastic.*

plate
a flat dish to eat food from *Take the plates into the kitchen.*

play
a story performed by actors in a theatre or on the radio The Tempest *is a play full of magical things.*

play (playing, played)
to do things that you like such as games or sports *Let's play outdoors.*

▼ play

playground
a place for children to play *There are swings and a slide at the playground.*

please
a word to use when you are asking for something politely *Please wait here.*

plenty
enough or more than enough *Have one of my sandwiches, I have plenty.*

A B C D E F G H I J K L M

plough

a piece of equipment that farmers use to turn the soil before they plant *Modern ploughs can cut through the earth very quickly.*

plug

1 a piece of plastic or rubber that stops water going out of a sink or bath *Put the plug in the bath, then turn on the water.*
2 a piece of plastic connected to an electrical wire that you put into a wall *Which one is the plug for the computer?*

plumber

a person whose job it is to fix water taps and pipes *The plumber repaired the leak.*

plus (pluses)

and, added to, the symbol + *Eleven plus six equals seventeen, 11 + 6 = 17.*

pocket

a small, flat bag sewn into a piece of clothing or luggage *Put your key in your pocket.*

poem

writing that uses words that sound good together. The words may rhyme *This poem is very funny.*

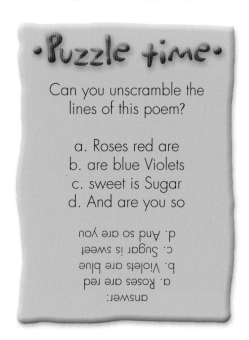

Puzzle time

Can you unscramble the lines of this poem?

a. Roses red are
b. are blue Violets
c. sweet is Sugar
d. And are you so

answer:
a. Roses are red
b. Violets are blue
c. Sugar is sweet
d. And so are you

point

1 a sharp end on something *Use a pencil with a sharp point.*
2 a certain place or time *There's a meeting point at the airport.*
3 the reason for something *The whole point was to raise money for the school.*
4 a mark for counting a score in a game *The answer is worth one point.*

point (pointing, pointed)

to use your hand or finger to show someone something *Point to where the gate is.*

pole

a long narrow piece of wood, plastic or metal *We forgot to take the tent poles.*

police

people whose job it is to make sure everyone obeys the law *Police officers work very hard.*

polite

speaking or acting in a pleasant and not rude way *It is polite to say please, thank you and excuse me.*

pond

a small area of water *There are fish in the pond.*

pony (ponies)

a small horse *Dusty is a beautiful little pony.*

▶ pony

pool

1 a place filled with water for swimming *I like playing in my pool when the weather is warm.*
2 a puddle or another small area of water *We saw tiny, coloured fish in the pools on the beach.*

A B C D E F G H I J K L M

poor

1 not having enough money *It's a very poor country.*
2 not as good as it should be *The food was poor.*

pop

1 a sudden noise *There was a loud pop when they opened the bottle.*
2 a short form of popular *They are a famous pop band.*
3 a fizzy drink *Do you want a bottle of pop?*

porcupine

a wild animal with long bristles on its back *Porcupine bristles are very sharp.*

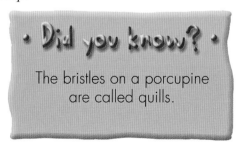

· Did you know? ·

The bristles on a porcupine are called quills.

porridge

a warm breakfast food that is made from oats *I like honey on porridge.*

post office

a place where people buy stamps and send letters *Can you get me some stamps at the post office?*

potato (potatoes)

a roundish white vegetable that grows under the ground *Potatoes have brown, yellow or red skins.*

pour (pouring, poured)

to make a liquid move out of or into something *Pour the juice while I make breakfast.*

powerful

1 having strength *A crocodile has powerful jaws.*
2 able to control *It is one of the most powerful countries in the world.*

N O P Q R S T U V W X Y Z

practice
Something that you do again and again to improve a skill *What time is swimming practice tonight?*

practise (practising, practised)
doing something regularly to improve a skill *Keep practising your serve.*

pram
a little bed on wheels for moving a baby around *We're taking the baby out in the pram.*

prepare (preparing, prepared)
to get ready or to make something ready *I'm preparing for the test.*

present
▶ present
1 a gift, a thing that you are given without asking for it *Thank you for all the presents.*
2 now *The story is set in the present.*

president
the leader of an organisation or a country *She is president of the club.*

press (pressing, pressed)
to push something *Press the space bar.*

pretend (pretending, pretended)
to act like something is true when it is not *She pretended to be asleep.*

pretty
pleasant to look at *What pretty flowers!*

price
the amount of money that something costs *The prices are high.*

prince
the son or grandson of a king or queen *Prince Charming found the glass slipper.*

A B C D E F G H I J K L M

princess (princesses)
a daughter or the granddaughter of a king or queen *The princess dreamed of a faraway place.*

◀ princess

print (printing, printed)
1 to put letters, numbers or pictures on paper with a machine *Print five copies of the story.*
2 to write words without joining the letters *Print your name in full.*

printer
1 a machine connected to a computer that makes copies on paper *The printer is out of paper.*
2 a person who runs a printing machine *Take the poster to the printer.*

prison
a place where people are kept under guard as punishment *The thief was sent to prison.*

prize
something that you win in a game or competition *First prize is a holiday.*

problem
1 something that is wrong and needs to be corrected *We have a problem.*
2 a question that needs to be answered *There are problems at work.*

promise (promising, promised)
to tell someone that you will definitely do something *The boy promised he would be good.*

protect (protecting, protected)
to take care of someone or something and not let it be hurt or damaged *Penguins protect their chicks.*

N O P Q R S T U V W X Y Z

proud

feeling happy that you or someone else has done something, or has something *My parents are proud of me.*

puddle

a little pool of water on the ground or floor *There are puddles after the rain.*

pull (pulling, pulled)

to move something towards you or drag something behind you *We pulled on the rope as hard as we could.*

◀ pull

pump

a machine that moves a liquid or gas in a certain direction *Take your tyre pump with you.*

puncture

a hole made by a sharp object, especially in a tyre *We had a puncture on the way home.*

punish (punishing, punished)

to do something bad or unpleasant to someone because they have done something wrong *Don't punish him, it was an accident.*

pupil

1 a school student *The pupils at school wear uniforms.*
2 the black circle in the middle of your eye *Your pupil gets smaller when you look at bright light.*

puppet

a toy that people move by putting their hand inside it or by pulling strings attached to it *There's a puppet show starting on the beach in ten minutes.*

A B C D E F G H I J K L M

puppy (puppies)
a young dog
Puppies love to play.

▶ puppies

pure
not mixed with
anything else *This is pure apple juice.*

purr
the soft, low sound a cat makes
when it is happy *Our cat purrs when
you scratch his ears.*

purse
a bag to keep money in *I'll have to
pay you later, I left my purse at home.*

push (pushing, pushed)
1 to move something away from
you or out of the way *He pushed past
everyone.*
2 to press down on something such
as a key or a button *Push the restart
button.*

put (putting, put)
to move a thing to a place *Just put
the bags over there.*

pyjamas
loose clothes that you wear to bed
Have a bath and put on your pyjamas.

pyramid
1 a very old stone building with
triangular walls that form a point
at the top *The Egyptian pyramids
were built 4000 years ago.*
2 something with this shape *The
tent is pyramid-shaped.*

▶ python

python
a large snake that kills animals for
food by squeezing them *Some
pythons grow to be 8 metres long.*

N O P Q R S T U V W X Y Z

quarter
one of four equal, or nearly equal, parts of something *Divide the apple into quarters.*

queen
the royal female ruler of a country or the wife of a king *The queen lives in a palace.*

▲ How many things can you see beginning with 'q'?

· **Did you know?** ·

Elizabeth I (the first) was queen of England from 1558 to 1603. She was the youngest daughter of Henry VIII (eighth).

◀ queen

question
something that you ask someone *We'll try to answer all your questions.*

queue
a line of people waiting *There was a long queue at the cinema.*

quick (quickly)
fast *Email is quick and easy.*

quiet (quietly)
1 not making a noise *Please be quiet.*
2 calm and still, not busy *The lake is quiet and peaceful this time of day.*

A B C D E F G H I J K L M

quilt

a warm cover for a bed *Patchwork quilts are made by sewing lots of small pieces of cloth together.*

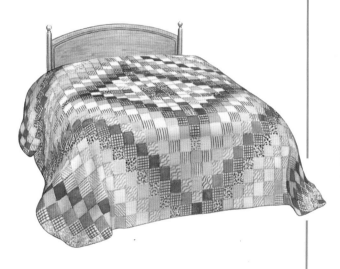

▲ quilt

quit (quitting, quit)

to stop doing something or to leave a computer program *To quit, press Ctrl + Q.*

quiz

a game or competition that tests your knowledge *We have a quiz night every year at Scouts.*

•Puzzle time•

Can you answer all the questions in this quiz?
1. What is a baby pig called?
2. Can penguins fly?
3. Is a tomato a fruit or a vegetable?
4. What are the spines on a porcupine called?

answers:
1. piglet 2. no 3. fruit 4. quills

quote (quoting, quoted)

to repeat the words that someone else has said or written *The English teacher quoted a line from Shakespeare's* Hamlet *to the class.*

N O P Q R S T U V W X Y Z

Rr

rabbit

a small furry animal with long ears *There are rabbits living in the wood.*

▶ rabbits

race

1 a competition to see who can do something the fastest *The race starts in 15 minutes.*
2 a group of people with similar physical features *The goal is that people of all races and all beliefs can live together happily.*

race (racing, raced)

1 to compete in a race *They're racing against some of the fastest runners in the world.*
2 to do something very quickly *Jessie raced through the first part of the test.*

racket (racquet)

1 a flat, hard net on the end of a stick that you use to play sports such as tennis, badminton and squash *These new tennis rackets are very light.*
2 noise *Who's making all that racket?*

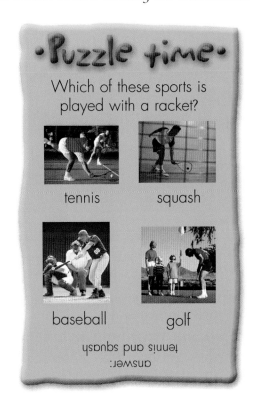

·Puzzle time·

Which of these sports is played with a racket?

tennis

squash

baseball

golf

answer:
tennis and squash

A B C D E F G H I J K L M

radio

a piece of equipment
that receives sounds
*I listen to the radio
every day.*

▶ radio

rail

1 a bar to hang things on or stop
things from falling *Put your wet towel
on the rail to dry.*
2 one of two metal tracks that a
train runs on *They put new rails all
along the track.*

railway

1 a train track *The railway runs to
the coast.*
2 a system of trains *A light railway
is being built in the city.*

rain

water that falls from clouds in the
sky *It's been raining all day.*

rainbow

the curve of colours that you see in
the sky after it rains and the sun
comes out *The colours of the rainbow
are red, orange, yellow, green, blue,
indigo and violet.*

raise (raising, raised)

to lift or put something in a higher
place *Raise your hand if you know the
answer.*

rat

an animal that looks like a big
mouse with a long tail *There are rats
in the barn*

▶ rat

rattle

a toy that makes a knocking noise
when you shake it *Babies like rattles.*

N O P Q R S T U V W X Y Z

raw
not cooked *You can eat cabbage raw.*

◀ read

read (reading, read)
to understand words or symbols printed on a page *I like reading in the garden.*

record (recording, recorded)
to write down, tape or otherwise store information *We recorded our voices on the computer.*

recycle (recycling, recycled)
to use something over again *We're recycling newspapers and magazines at school.*

reflection
an image, like a copy of something, that is seen in a mirror or water *We could see the reflection of the mountain in the water.*

refrigerator (fridge)
a machine to keep food cool *Put the milk back in the refrigerator.*

▶ refrigerator

remember (remembering, remembered)
1 to keep information about the past in your mind *I remember how much fun we had then.*
2 to bring back information to your mind *I just remembered, I'm away then.*

remind (reminding, reminded)
to cause someone to remember something *Remind me to buy sugar.*

A B C D E F G H I J K L M

repeat (repeating, repeated)
to say or do something again *Sorry, could you repeat that – I didn't hear you.*

rescue (rescuing, rescued)
to save someone or something from danger *The lifeguard rescued the children.*

▶ rhinoceros

rest (resting, rested)
to not be active, to relax *I wasn't asleep, just resting.*

restaurant
a place where people eat and pay for meals *There's a new Thai restaurant in town.*

result
1 something that happens because of something else *This beautiful garden is the result of a lot of hard work.*
2 a final score *Have you heard the latest football results?*

return (returning, returned)
1 to come back or go back to a place *He returned after the meeting.*
2 to give or send something back *We returned the books to the library.*

rhinoceros (rhinoceroses)
a very large, wild animal with thick skin and a large horn on its nose *Rhinoceroses have very weak eyesight.*

rhyme (rhyming, rhymed)
when a word ends with the same sound as another word *Tree rhymes with three.*

▼ ribbon

ribbon
a narrow piece of cloth or paper for tying up presents or decorating things *What colour ribbon is on your dress?*

rice

grains from a plant that are boiled and eaten as food *We had pilau rice with our vegetable curry.*

rich

1 having a lot of money *We are not rich but we're very happy.*
2 food that has butter, cream and eggs is rich food *The cheese sauce is too rich for me!*
3 a deep or strong colour, smell or sound *The queen was wearing rich, purple robes.*

riddle

a difficult but funny question *Tom knows lots of riddles.*

ride (riding, rode, ridden)

to travel on and control the movement of a bicycle or a horse *Dad is teaching my little sister how to ride a bike.*

right

correct *You got all the answers right!*

▲ How many things can you see beginning with 'r'?

ring

1 a piece of jewellery worn on the finger *That's a pretty silver ring.*
2 a circle or something that is the shape of a circle *We put our chairs in a ring around the teacher.*
3 the sound made by a bell *The phone has a very loud ring.*
4 a telephone call *Give me a ring when you get home from work.*

river

a long line of water that flows to the sea *The Nile is the longest river.*

road

a track for vehicles such as cars and trucks to travel on *Some country roads are very narrow.*

roar

the sound a lion makes *There was a loud roar just outside the tent.*

robot

a machine that can do things that a person can do *My robot can play football.*

▶ robot

rock

1 the hard, stony part of the Earth's surface *They drilled through rock to find the oil.*
2 a large stone *We sat on the rocks and fished.*
3 a type of music that has a strong beat *My brother likes hard rock.*

rocket

1 a space vehicle shaped like a tube *The rocket is carrying valuable equipment to the space station.*
2 a tube-shaped firework *Rockets were exploding all over the sky.*

roll (rolling, rolled)

to move by turning over *The ball rolled across the pitch.*

roof

the outer covering over the top of a building or car *Rain leaked through the roof and onto the floor.*

room

part of a building that has its own floor, walls and ceiling *What's your room like?*

  ▶ rope

rope

very thick string *Tie the rope tightly.*

N O P Q R S T U V W X Y Z

rose

a flower that grows on a stem with thorns *My mother loves roses.*

▲ roses

rough

1 uneven, not smooth *That bench is quite rough.*
2 not gentle *Don't be rough with the puppy.*

roundabout

1 a round place where roads meet *Turn left at the next roundabout.*
2 a round playground toy that children spin and ride on *Let's ride on the roundabout.*

route

the way to go to a place *We looked at the map and decided which route to take.*

row (rowing, rowed)

to move a small boat through water using long wooden poles that are wide at one end *We rowed the boat across the lake.*

royal

of or belonging to a queen or king *The people cheered as the royal procession marched through the town.*

rubber

1 a bouncy material that is made from the juice of a tree *Car tyres are made of rubber.*
2 a small object that is used for taking pencil marks off paper *I've made lots of mistakes on my homework, can I borrow your rubber?*

A B C D E F G H I J K L M

rubbish

1 paper and other things that are no longer needed *Rubbish goes in the bin.*
2 something that is bad, wrong or silly *The film was rubbish.*

Did you know?

Recycling rubbish such as paper and glass is good for the environment.

rude

speaking or acting in a way that makes people feel bad *Don't be rude.*

rug

1 a small carpet *The cat is on the rug.*
2 a blanket *Put the rug over your feet.*

rule

a law or guide about how something must be done *It's wrong to break the rules at school.*

ruler

1 a long, flat piece of plastic or wood that has a straight edge and measurements *I use a ruler in maths.*
2 a person who has power over a country *The country has no ruler.*

▶ run

run (running, ran)

1 to move your legs faster than when you are walking *Run as fast as you can!*
2 to control *The business is run from home.*
3 to make a piece of equipment or a computer program work *Run the computer program.*

N O P Q R S T U V W X Y Z

Ss

sad

unhappy *What's happened? You look so sad.*

safe

not dangerous *Home is where you feel good and safe.*

sail

a large piece of strong material attached to a boat or ship, which catches the wind and makes the boat move across the water *The ship has many sails.*

▶ sails

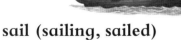

sail (sailing, sailed)

to travel across water in a boat or ship *I am learning to sail a boat.*

salad

vegetables or fruit mixed together, usually eaten raw *We'll have a mixed salad.*

▶ salad

salt

very tiny grains that come from sea water and rocks, that are put on food to make it taste good *This needs a little more salt.*

same

not different or changed *Look, our clothes are exactly the same.*

sand

tiny pieces of crushed rock *The beach is covered in beautiful, white sand.*

sandwich (sandwiches)

two pieces of bread with cheese, meat or vegetables in between *We'll make some sandwiches for the picnic.*

A B C D E F G H I J K L M

• Puzzle time •

Can you put these sandwich instructions in the right order?

a. Next, spread one side of each slice with butter.

b. Put the cheese on one slice of bread.

c. Now put the other slice on top.

d. First, take two slices of bread.

e. Eat your sandwich

answer:
d, a, b, e

saucer
the small dish that goes under a cup *We put some milk in a saucer for the kittens.*

sausage
a mixture of meat, cereal and spices that is shaped like a tube *Would you like sausages with your breakfast?*

scales
a machine that is used for weighing things *Weigh the ingredients on the scales.*

scar
the mark left on your skin after a cut has healed *I have a scar above my left eye.*

scare (scaring, scared)
to frighten *This film will really scare you!*

scarecrow
an object that is made to look like a person, which is put in fields to scare off birds so they don't eat the crops *We've made our scarecrow out of straw.*

scared
feeling afraid, frightened *Please leave a light on, I'm scared of the dark.*

school

the place where children go to study and be taught *I'm studying French at school.*

science

the study of information about the world *Biology, physics and chemistry are all kinds of science.*

score (scoring, scored)

to get points in a game *Goal! Goal! We've scored another goal!*

scorpion

an animal that has eight legs and a tail *Scorpions have a painful sting.*

Did you know?
Scorpions have been around for 4 million years.

◀ scorpion

scratch (scratching, scratched)

1 to rub your skin with your fingers or nails *Don't scratch your face.*
2 to damage an object by rubbing it with something *The car is scratched.*

▲ How many things can you see beginning with 's'?

scream (screaming, screamed)

to make a loud noise when you are afraid, angry or hurt *She screamed loudly.*

screen

1 the flat part of a computer or television that you look at *You're too close to the screen.*
2 a flat piece of material for showing films *The cinema has a screen.*

A B C D E F G H I J K L M

sea

a large area of salty water, sometimes called the ocean *Look, you can see the sea from here.*

seal

1 an animal that lives in the sea and eats fish *Seals are good swimmers and can dive underwater for a long time.*
2 wax, plastic or paper that you break to open a container or a document *Do not buy this product if the seal is broken.*

▼ seals

secret

something that you do not want other people to know *Please don't tell anyone else – it's a secret.*

see (seeing, saw, seen)

1 to use your eyes to look *We saw a deer.*
2 to understand *See? This is how it works.*
3 to watch *Did you see that programme on TV last night?*
4 to meet or visit someone *We went to see Chloe in hospital.*

seed

the part of a plant that a new plant grows from *Put the seeds in the ground.*

seesaw

a long board that is balanced in the middle so that the ends go up and down *There's a seesaw in the playground.*

send (sending, sent)

to make something go or be taken to another place *I sent her an email yesterday.*

sew (sewing, sewed, sewn)
to join cloth together with a needle and thread *I'll sew the button on for you.*

shade
1 where the sun is not shining *Sit in the shade of the umbrella.*
2 a thing to stop light *Can you pull the shade down, please?*
3 a colour *That's a nice shade of green.*

shake (shaking, shook, shaken)
to move something up and down or side to side quickly *Shake well before opening.*

shampoo
liquid soap for washing your hair *Did you bring the shampoo?*

shape
the outline or form of a thing *What shape is it?*

shark
a large fish that usually has sharp teeth *Some sharks can be dangerous to humans.*

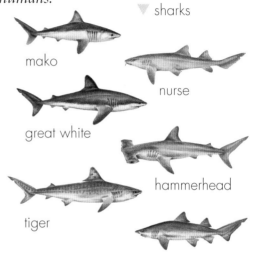

▼ sharks

mako

nurse

great white

hammerhead

tiger

sand

sheep (sheep)
a farm animal kept for wool and meat *There are sheep on the hill.*

shelf (shelves)
a board, usually wooden, fixed on a wall for putting things on *Can you reach that shelf?*

shell

the hard covering of an egg, a seed or an animal such as a turtle or a crab *Ostrich eggs are very big and have thick shells.*

ship

a large boat *The pirates filled the ship with treasure.*

▶ ship

shirt

a piece of clothing worn on the top half of your body *Tuck your shirt in.*

shock

1 a bad surprise *The bill was quite a shock.*
2 a pain you feel when electricity goes through your body *I got a shock from that plug!*

shoe

one of the things made of strong material that you wear on your feet *Wear comfortable shoes.*

shoot (shooting, shot)

1 to fire a weapon at someone or something *Don't shoot!*
2 to kick or throw a ball into a goal or net in a game *Shoot when you are closer to the basket.*

N O P Q R S T U V W X Y Z

shop

a place that sells things *What time does the shop open?*

short

1 not tall *He is short for his age.*
2 not long *She cut her hair short.*
3 not lasting a long time *Let's take a short break.*

shorts

short trousers *We wear our shorts in summer.*

▶ shorts

shoulder

the top of your arm where it joins your body *Put the bag over your shoulder.*

shout (shouting, shouted)

to call out to someone in a loud voice *There's no need to shout at me, I'm right here!*

show (showing, showed)

1 to let someone see something *Show me your new game.*
2 to guide someone somewhere or help them to do something *The guide showed us around.*

shower

1 something that you stand under to wash your body *Every room in the hotel has been fitted with a private shower.*
2 a light fall of rain *There will be showers in the afternoon.*

shrink (shrinking, shrank, shrunk)

to become smaller *My favourite skirt shrank in the wash.*

A B C D E F G H I J K L M

shut (shutting, shut)
to close *Shut the door, please.*

sideways
towards one side, not forwards or backwards *Turn sideways and then you can get past.*

sign (signing, signed)
to write your name on something *Sign at the bottom.*

silly
stupid, not reasonable *Don't be so silly!*

sing (singing, sang, sung)
to make music with your voice *Sing us a song.*

sink (sinking, sank, sunk)
to go down below the surface of water *The ship* Titanic *sank after it hit an iceberg.*

sister
a girl or woman who has the same parents as you *Julie is my younger sister.*

sit (sitting, sat)
to put your bottom on a chair or another type of seat *I must sit down, my feet ache.*

▼ skate

skate (skating, skated)
to move over ground or ice wearing boots with wheels or blades *He can skate well.*

skeleton
the bones in your body *He wore a suit with a skeleton painted on it for Hallowe'en.*

sketch (sketching, sketched)
to draw quickly *Artists sketch a scene first.*

▶ ski

ski (skiing, skied)
to move quickly over snow or water on long, narrow pieces of wood *Do you know how to ski?*

skirt
a piece of clothing worn by girls and women that hangs from the waist down *You can wear that skirt to school.*

sky (skies)
the space above you where the Sun, Moon, stars and clouds are *The sky was full of stars.*

slap (slapping, slapped)
to hit something with an open hand *She slapped his hand.*

sled (sledges)
a vehicle or toy for moving across ice or snow *We built a sled out of an old wooden box.*

sleep (sleeping, slept)
to not be awake *The baby is sleeping.*

▶ sleep

A B C D E F G H I J K L M

slide (sliding, slid)
to move across or down a smooth surface *The car slid across the ice.*

slippers
shoes that you wear indoors *Put your slippers on if your feet are cold.*

slow (slow)
not fast, taking a long time *This is a slow train.*

small
little or young *The jeans have a small pocket for coins.*

smile (smiling, smiled)
to make your mouth curve up and look happy *Why are you smiling?*

smoke
the cloudy gas that is made when something burns *The room filled with smoke.*

smooth
not rough or bumpy *You can skate on the pavement, it's smooth.*

snail
an animal that looks like a worm with a shell on its back *We have a lot of snails in our garden.*

Did you know?
The biggest snail ever found was an African giant snail – it was the size of a football!

snake
an animal that has a long body with no legs *Simon has a pet snake.*

sneeze (sneezing, sneezed)
to blow air out of your nose suddenly, with a loud noise *He's sneezing and coughing because he has a cold.*

snow

soft pieces of frozen water that fall from the sky *The trees are covered in snow.*

▼ snow

soap

something that you use with water to wash your body *Get a new bar of soap.*

soccer

football, a game played by two teams that try to get a round ball between two posts *A soccer team has 11 players.*

socks

pieces of clothing that you wear on your feet *Socks keep your feet warm.*

sofa

a long, soft seat for two or more people *Shall we sit on the sofa?*

▲ socks

soft

1 not hard *This bed is soft.*
2 not loud *She has a soft voice.*
3 smooth to touch *The rabbit has lovely, soft fur.*

software

the programs that run on a computer *He designs software.*

solid

hard, not a liquid or a gas, without spaces inside *The front door is made of solid wood.*

A B C D E F G H I J K L M

some
1 an amount of something that is not exact *Would you like some rice with your dinner?*
2 part of, but not all *Some of these apples are rotten.*

son
a male child *My daughter is at the same school as your son.*

song
a piece of music *The children sang songs in the school hall.*

sore
hurting or painful *Is the cut on your leg still sore?*

sorry
feeling bad and wanting to apologise for something you have done *Did she say sorry for making you late for work?*

soup
a liquid food made from meat or vegetables *Have a bowl of tomato soup.*

▶ soup

sour
having a taste like lemons, not sweet *This juice is sour.*

space
1 an empty or open place *Is there any space left?*
2 everything beyond the Earth's air *Space travel is very exciting.*

spade
a tool for digging *Turn the soil with a spade.*

spaghetti
long, thin strips of pasta *Ella likes spaghetti.*

speed
how fast something moves *At what speed are we travelling?*

spell (spelling, spelled)
to write or say the letters of a word in the correct order *How do you spell 'skateboard'?*

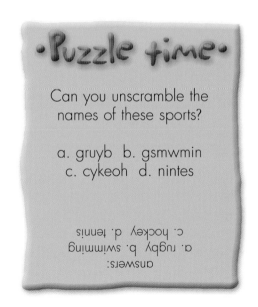

▶ spider

spider
a small animal with eight legs *There's a spider in the bath.*

spill (spilling, spilled, spilt)
to cause a liquid to fall to the ground accidentally *I spilled the drink on the carpet.*

.

spoon
an object with a handle and small bowl that is used for eating *Put the spoon to the right of the plate.*

sport
physical activities such as swimming and tennis *Swimming is a sport the whole family likes.*

▼ sport

•Puzzle time•

Can you unscramble the names of these sports?

a. gruyb b. gsmwmin
c. cykeoh d. nintes

answers:
a. rugby b. swimming
c. hockey d. tennis

A B C D E F G H I J K L M

spring
the time of year between winter and summer *The cherry tree flowers in spring.*

squirrel
a small wild animal with a long, bushy tail *Squirrels are very good at climbing trees.*

stairs
steps in a building that go from one floor to another *I'll take the stairs to the office.*

▶ stars

stamp
1 a piece of paper that you buy to put on a letter or postcard before you post it *I'd like a first class stamp.*
2 a thing you put ink on and then press onto something to make a mark *The letter has a stamp on it.*

stand (standing, stood)
to be on your feet *She's standing by the door.*

star
1 a ball of burning gas that looks like a light in the sky *The stars are bright tonight*
2 a famous person *She's a big star now.*
3 a shape with five or six points *We baked biscuits shaped like stars.*

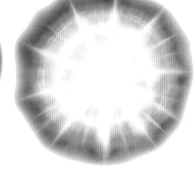

starfish (starfishes)
a star-shaped animal that lives in the sea *Starfish move very slowly.*

start (starting, started)
to begin *I think it's time we made a start on the decorating.*

stay (staying, stayed)
1 to not leave a place *You stay here, I'll be right back.*
2 to live in a place for a short amount of time *When I was little, we stayed at my aunt's house every summer.*
3 to continue to remain the same *He's never grumpy, his mood stays the same all the time.*

steal (stealing, stole, stolen)
to take something that doesn't belong to you *The thieves stole my dad's car.*

stick
a long, thin piece of wood *We managed to make a fire by rubbing two sticks together.*

▷ stomach

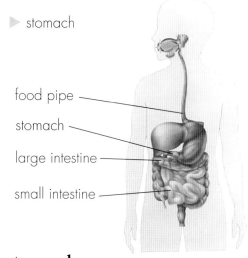

food pipe

stomach

large intestine

small intestine

stomach
the part inside your body where food goes when you eat *Another word for stomach is tummy.*

stone
1 rock *There is a stone floor in the castle.*
2 fourteen pounds or 6.35 kilograms *What is your weight in stones?*
3 the seed in some fruits *Careful, the cherries have stones in them.*

A B C D E F G H I J K L M

stool
a seat with no back *Sit on the stool.*

stop (stopping, stopped)
1 to quit doing something *Stop talking for a minute.*
2 to quit moving *Stop for the red light.*
3 to prevent something happening *The teacher stopped the fight.*

story (stories)
a description of events that may be real or imaginary *Everyone knows the story of Peter Pan.*

· Did you know? ·
The story of Peter Pan was written by J.M. Barrie in 1902.

straight not crooked or bent *She has very straight hair.*

strange
1 unusual *He's a strange-looking man.*
2 unfamiliar *He told a very strange story.*

strawberry strawberry (strawberries)
a soft, heart-shaped red fruit *You can pick the strawberries yourself on some farms.*

▶ strawberries

stream
a small river *We drank water from a mountain stream.*

stretch (stretching, stretched)
1 to get longer or bigger *Tights can stretch quite a bit.*
2 to straighten parts of your body *She stretched her legs out under the table.*

string

thick thread or thin rope *Tie some string around the box.*

◀ string

strong

1 powerful *Climbers have strong legs.*
2 not easily broken or damaged *The metal case is very strong.*

stupid

not sensible or clever *What a stupid idea!*

submarine

a ship that can travel underwater *Submarines can help us to find out about underwater life.*

sudden

happening quickly and unexpectedly *There was a sudden explosion.*

sugar

a sweet substance used to flavour food *Sugar is made from plants.*

suitcase

a case or bag to carry clothes in when you travel *We have a suitcase with wheels.*

summer

the time of year between spring and autumn *Are you going on holiday this summer?*

Sun

▶ Sun

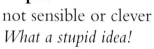

the very bright star that the Earth travels around *All the planets in the Solar System travel around the Sun.*

A B C D E F G H I J K L M

supermarket
a large shop that sells food and other things *The supermarket stays open late on Fridays.*

surprise
something that is completely unexpected *An email from you! What a nice surprise!*

sweep (sweeping, swept)
to brush dirt from the floor or ground *Have you swept the kitchen?*

sweet
1 tasting sugary *These strawberries are very sweet.*
2 nice or pleasant *That's a sweet thing to say.*

swim (swimming, swam, swum)
to move through or across water by using your arms and legs *I can swim a whole length of the pool.*

▲ swing

swing (swinging, swung)
to move backwards, forwards or from side to side from a fixed point *I like swinging, it's lots of fun.*

sword
a very large knife that is used for fighting *'Excalibur' is the name of a famous sword.*

N O P Q R S T U V W X Y Z

T-shirt/t-shirt

a shirt with short sleeves, no collar and no buttons *Put a T-shirt on, it's warm today.*

table

1 a piece of furniture with legs and a flat top *Please clear the table.*

2 a list of things such as numbers or words arranged in rows and columns *There's a table of prices and times.*

▲ table

tail

the part of an animal at the end of its back *The dog has a long, white tail.*

◀ tail

take (taking, took, taken)

1 to carry something *Take an umbrella.*

2 to move something or someone to another place *Take this note to Mrs. Burnett.*

3 to steal *The thieves took all the money.*

talk (talking, talked)

to speak *Who were you talking to on the telephone last night?*

tall

1 higher than normal *My Grandad is tall, I am short.*

2 having a certain height *The fence is one metre tall.*

tank

1 a container for liquids *There's a leak in the petrol tank.*

2 a large fighting vehicle *Tanks are used in wars.*

A B C D E F G H I J K L M

tap
something that controls the flow of a liquid or gas *Turn the tap off.*

tape
1 a long, flat, narrow piece of plastic used for recording sounds or images, or the plastic container it is in *Can I borrow the tape?*
2 flat, narrow plastic that is sticky on one side *Put some tape on the package.*

taste (tasting, tasted)
1 to have a flavour *What does the soup taste like?*
2 to try a little food or drink to see what it is like *Have you tasted the pizza?*

taxi
a car that takes people to different places, for money *We'll take a taxi.*

tea
1 leaves that are used to make a drink or the drink made from these leaves *Pour the tea.*
2 the evening meal *What's for tea?*

teacher
a person who gives lessons in a subject *Kate's an art teacher.*

team
1 a group of people who play a game together *Which team are you on?*
2 a group of people who work together on a project *We have a great team.*

tear
a drop of water that comes out of your eye *Tears ran down his face.*

◀ taxi

N O P Q R S T U V W X Y Z

tear (tearing, tore, torn)
to rip, split or make a hole in
something *Tear the paper in half.*

teddy
a toy animal that looks like a bear
My teddy is soft and cuddly.

telephone
a piece of equipment that you use to
speak to someone in another place
Where's your telephone?

▶ telescope

telescope
a piece of equipment that
you use to look at things
that are far away *Look
through the telescope.*

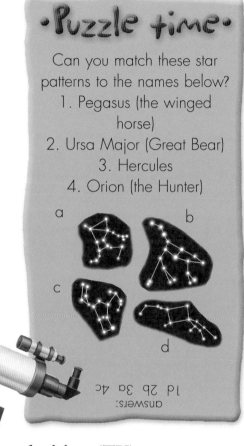

•Puzzle time•

Can you match these star
patterns to the names below?
1. Pegasus (the winged
horse)
2. Ursa Major (Great Bear)
3. Hercules
4. Orion (the Hunter)

a   b

c

d

answers:
1d 2b 3a 4c

television (TV)
a machine that shows
programmes *What's on television?*

A B C D E F G H I J K L M

tell (telling, told)
1 to pass on information *I told you that story yesterday.*
2 to understand *I can't tell what it means.*

◀ tennis

tennis
a game played by two or four people who hit a ball over a net to score points *Tennis is a very fast game.*

tent
a temporary house, made of cloth or plastic, that is used for camping *The tent will keep us dry.*

terrible
very bad *That's terrible!*

test
1 a set of questions to measure knowledge *You must study carefully for the test.*
2 a set of checks to find out if something is safe or good to use *Cars must pass several tests.*

thank (thanking, thanked)
to tell someone you are pleased about something they have given you or have done for you *Remember to thank them.*

theatre
a building where you can go and see plays *Shall we go to the theatre this weekend?*

thick
1 not thin *The entrance was covered by a thick sheet of plastic.*
2 not watery *Make a thick paste from flour and water.*

thief (thieves)

a person who steals *The bank was robbed by a gang of thieves.*

▲ How many things can you see beginning with 't'?

thin

1 having not much distance from one side to the other *Cut the paper into thin strips.*
2 not fat *She's quite thin.*
3 watery *It's a thin, clear soup.*

think (thinking, thought)

1 to use your mind to consider or remember something *Let me think.*
2 to have an opinion, to believe *I think we should try it.*

thirsty

feeling that you need to drink something *Are you thirsty?*

through

from one side to the other *Look through the window.*

throw (throwing, threw)

to make something go through the air *Throw the ball through the net.*

thumb

the finger on the inside of your hand *I've cut my thumb.*

thunder

the loud noise you can hear during a storm *As the storm broke we heard a very loud clap of thunder.*

ticket

a piece of paper that shows you have paid *I have tickets for the game.*

A B C D E F G H I J K L M

tidy
neat and organised *Mandy's room is never tidy.*

tie (tying, tied)
to join pieces of string, rope or thread together *Tie your shoelaces up.*

tiger
a large, wild cat that has black stripes on its yellow fur *The tiger's coat is black and orange.*

tight
1 close-fitting *That looks a bit tight.*
2 firmly in place *Is it shut tight?*

tights
clothing worn on the legs *I wear tights to ballet.*

timetable
a list of things and the time they happen *Check the timetable.*

tired
feeling that you need to rest *The baby is tired.*

toast
bread that has been cooked in a toaster or a grill *I'll make some toast for breakfast.*

today
this day *What's the date today?*

· Did you know? ·
Tigers are the biggest members of the cat family.

▶ tiger

N O P Q R S T U V W X Y Z

toe

one of the five parts of your body at the end of your foot *Ouch, I stubbed my toe.*

together

1 joined or mixed *Mix the eggs and milk together.*
2 with each other *Shall we go together?*

toilet

lavatory *Where's the toilet?*

tomato (tomatoes)

a red fruit that can be eaten raw or cooked *Put tomatoes in the salad.*

◀ tomatoes

tool

a piece of equipment that you use to do a job *Hammers and saws are tools.*

tooth (teeth)

one of the hard, white things in your mouth *You should brush your teeth twice a day.*

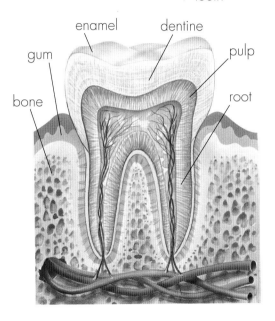

▼ tooth

enamel

dentine

gum

pulp

bone

root

tongue

the soft part of your body that is inside your mouth that you use to speak with and to taste things *The ice cream feels cold on my tongue.*

A B C D E F G H I J K L M

top

1 the highest part of something
I've hidden the presents on top of the wardrobe.
2 a toy that balances on a point
Let's spin the top.
3 a cover for the upper body *That's a pretty top.*
4 a cover for a container *Put the top back on.*

torch

a light powered by batteries *Shine the torch over here.*

tortoise

a land animal that can pull its head and legs into the shell that covers its body *Tortoises can only move very slowly.*

touch (touching, touched)

1 to put your fingers or hand on something *Please don't touch the paintings.*
2 to be so close to another thing that there is no space between the two *The wires are touching.*

towel

a cloth that you use to dry things or your body with *Dry your hands on the towel.*

town

a place with houses and other buildings where people live and work *Our town has a good selection of shopping facilities.*

◀ toy

toy

something that children like to play with *Can I play with my toy plane?*

N O P Q R S T U V W X Y Z

tractor
a big vehicle that is used on a farm
Tractors are very powerful.

traffic lights
lights where two or more roads meet
that change colour, telling you
when to stop and go *Turn
left at the traffic lights.*

train
a line of
carriages pulled
by an engine on a
track *Trains travel at a fast speed.*

◀ train

trainers
sports shoes *I bought some new trainers.*

**transport (transporting,
transported)**
to move people or things from one
place to another *The tanker transports
fuel.*

trap (trapping, trapped)
to catch something in a piece of
equipment *It traps mice.*

**travel (travelling,
travelled)**
to go from one place to another
They're travelling by car.

treasure
a collection of valuable things
The chest is filled with treasure.

tree
a large, tall plant with a trunk and
branches *It's fun to climb trees.*

trick
1 something done to entertain
people *That was a clever trick.*
2 something done to fool or cheat
someone *That was a mean trick.*

A B C D E F G H I J K L M

trip (tripping, tripped)
to catch your foot on something, to stumble *Be careful – you could trip on the step.*

trip
a journey *We've decided to go on a trip around the world.*

trousers
clothing that covers the legs *He's wearing grey trousers.*

▶ truck

truck
a vehicle for carrying loads *We were stuck behind a truck.*

trunk
1 the main part of a tree *Palm trees have thick trunks.*
2 an elephant's nose *The elephant has a long trunk.*
3 a box for storing things in *Where's the key for this trunk?*

try (trying tried)
1 to make an effort *I tried to ring you.*
2 to test or sample something *Have you tried the pasta?*

tunnel
a long hole underground *There is a secret tunnel.*

turn
1 to move so you are looking or going in a new direction *Turn away.*
2 to move something to a different position *Turn the dial.*

turtle
an animal that lives in water that can pull its head and legs into the shell on its back *Turtles are reptiles.*

Uu

ugly

not nice to look at *What an ugly colour!*

umbrella

a piece of equipment made of cloth stretched over a frame that keeps the rain off *It's raining outside – I'll take my umbrella.*

▲ umbrella

uncle

your mother's or father's brother, or your aunt's husband *He looks like his uncle.*

under

below, to a lower place *Put your bag under your seat.*

understand (understanding, understood)

1 to know the meaning of words or ideas *Does he understand English?*
2 to know how something works *Doctors understand the disease.*
3 to know how and why someone feels or acts a certain way *You don't understand.*

• Did you know? •

You can understand words from other languages. From Italian we get the words balcony, giraffe and violin. From Spanish we get banana and guitar. From French we get chocolate, crocodile and medicine.

underwear

pieces of clothing that you wear next to your body, under your other clothes *Pack some underwear.*

▲ How many things can you see beginning with 'u'?

unhappy

not happy, sad *Cheer up, try not to look so unhappy.*

▶ unhappy

▲ uniforms

uniform

clothes worn by everyone in a group of people *Everyone wore uniforms.*

up

towards a higher position *Pass that brush up to me.*

upset

1 feeling worried, sad or angry *I didn't mean to upset you.*
2 feeling sick *His stomach is upset.*

upstairs

towards or on the upper floors of a building *Take these papers upstairs.*

N O P Q R S T U V W X Y Z

Vv

valley
the low land between two hills *There is a river in the valley.*

van
a small truck *The delivery van is here.*

vanish (vanishing, vanished)
to disappear *The deer suddenly vanished.*

vase
a container to hold water in *The vase is hand-painted.*

vegetable
a plant grown for food *Vegetables are healthy foods.*

vehicle
a machine which carries people or things *Trucks and trains are vehicles.*

vest
an undershirt *Put a vest on, it's cold today.*

vet (veterinary surgeon)
an animal doctor *The vet is treating our dog.*

▶ vet

▼ vase

video (video cassette recorder)
a machine for recording or playing TV programmes *Switch the video on.*

village
a group of houses and buildings in the country *It's a beautiful old village.*

A B C D E F G H I J K L M

vinegar
a liquid that is used to preserve food, or add flavour *Put vinegar on your chips.*

violin
a musical instrument that is played with a bow *My brother is learning to play the violin.*

▶ violin

virus (viruses)
1 a very tiny living thing that causes disease and illness *Flu is caused by a virus.*
2 a computer program that can damage files *The virus has damaged my files.*

visit (visiting, visited)
to go to see a person or a place *You can visit us this evening.*

voice
the sounds a person makes when speaking or singing *I didn't recognise your voice.*

volcano (volcanoes)
a mountain with an opening that sprays out steam or lava *The volcano is very active.*

vote (voting, voted)
to show which idea or person you choose by raising your hand or writing on paper *Let's take a vote on this idea.*

How many things can you see beginning with 'v'?

N O P Q R S T U V W X Y Z

Ww

waiter
a man or woman who serves food in a restaurant or café *Call the waiter, I want to pay.*

▶ waiter

waitress
a woman who serves food in a restaurant or café *Ask the waitress for the bill.*

wake (waking, woke, woken)
to stop being asleep *Wake up!*

walk (walking, walked)
to move along, putting one foot in front of the other *Let's walk together*

wall
1 the sides of a room or a building *There are several pictures on the wall.*
2 a structure made of stone or brick that divides a space *There's a brick wall around the garden.*

wand
a magic stick that fairies, witches and magicians use to do magic tricks *She waved her wand and turned the pumpkin into a coach.*

want (wanting, wanted)
to wish, desire or need something *Do you want a sandwich?*

wardrobe
a cupboard to hang clothes in *It's a big wardrobe.*

warm
slightly hot, not cool or cold *The water is lovely and warm.*

wash (washing, washed)
to clean with water *Wash your face.*

▶ wasp

wasp
a black and yellow flying insect that stings *Wasps live in nests.*

wastepaper bin
a container to put unwanted paper and rubbish in *Empty the wastepaper bin.*

watch
a small clock that you wear on your wrist *I'd like a watch for my birthday.*

watch (watching, watched)
to look at something and pay attention *We're watching TV.*

water
a liquid that falls from the sky as rain *Have a glass of water.*

waterfall
water from a stream or a river that falls straight down over rocks *There is a pool under the waterfall.*

wave
1 a raised part of moving water on the sea *Waves crashed on the beach.*
2 a movement of your hand to say goodbye, hello or get someone's attention *Give them a wave.*
3 the way light and sound move *Sound is carried on radio waves.*

▲ wave

weak
not strong *I feel weak and dizzy.*

wear (wearing, wore)
to have something, such as clothes, on your body *What shall I wear to the party?*

weather
the condition of the air – how hot or cold it is, the wind, rain and clouds *What's the weather like today?*

web
1 the very thin strings a spider weaves *A spider catches food in its web.*
2 the World Wide Web on the Internet *Do you use the Web?*

week
seven days *See you next week!*

weigh (weighing, weighed)
1 to measure how heavy something is *Weigh the fruit.*
2 to be heavy or light *How much do you weigh?*

well
1 in a good way *Well done!*
2 healthy, not ill *Get well soon.*

wet
not dry *Your hair's still wet.*

whale
a very large sea animal *Whales are mammals, not fish.*

▲ whale

wheel
a round object that turns and moves a vehicle along *The wheel came off the bike.*

whisper (whispering, whispered)
to speak very quietly so other people can't hear *Whisper the secret to me.*

A B C D E F G H I J K L M

whistle (whistling, whistled)
to blow air out through your lips
and make a sound *Can you whistle?*

wicked
very bad or evil *The wicked witch
trapped them.*

wife (wives)
the woman that a man is married to
His wife is very nice.

win (winning, won)
to be the first or the best in a race or
other competition *He's won the race!*

◀ win

wind
air moving across the ground *The
wind is strong.*

window
a glass-covered opening in a
building *Look out of the window.*

▲ winter

winter
the time of year between autumn
and spring *The weather can be very cold
in winter.*

wish (wishing, wished)
to hope for or want something *What
did you wish for?*

witch (witches)

a woman who is supposed to have magic powers *The witches huddled over their big, black pot, making spells.*

• Did you know? •

Witches have been around for hundreds of years. Witchcraft was once an ancient religion. Modern witches do exist, but they don't fly around on broomsticks!

wizard

a man who is supposed to have magic powers *The wizard broke the spell.*

wolf (wolves)

a wild animal that looks like a large dog *They heard the wolf howling at the moon.*

woman (women)

a female adult *Are there women on the team?*

wonder (wondering, wondered)

to think about something and why it is that way *I wonder why she said that?*

wood

1 the material that a tree is made of *Put more wood on the fire.*
2 a small forest *We walked through the wood.*

wool

1 hair that grows on animals, such as sheep. *The wool is thick and warm.*
2 thread made from animal's hair *Get me a ball of wool.*

◀ wizard

A B C D E F G H I J K L M

work (working, worked)
1 to do a job *Does she enjoy her work as a doctor?*
2 to go or operate smoothly *This machine is working properly now.*

•Puzzle time•

Match the workers with the things they need to do their jobs

A
actor
artist
pilot
waiter

B
paint
theatre
menu
plane

answers: actor/theatre artist/paint pilot/plane waiter/menu

world
the Earth, the planet that we live on and everything that is on it *The Nile is the longest river in the world.*

worm
a long, thin animal with no legs that lives in earth *Worms are good for the soil.*

▶ worm

worry (worrying, worried)
to have the feeling that something bad might happen *You shouldn't worry, it's not a problem.*

worse (worst)
less than good *My cold is worse.*

write (writing, wrote)
1 to make a new story, poem, play, song or book *I wrote her a letter.*
2 to make letters, numbers and words *Write your name in the diary.*

wrong
not right, incorrect *We've made a wrong turn.*

X-ray

1 a beam of energy that can go through solid things *X-rays are used at airports.*

2 a photograph of the inside of the body *The X-ray shows that his hand may be broken.*

How many things can you see beginning with 'x', 'y' and 'z'?

▶ xylophone

xylophone

a musical instrument that is played by hitting flat, wooden or metal bars with a pair of sticks *The word xylophone comes from the Greek words 'xylo' (wood) and 'phone' (sound).*

yacht

a sailing boat *Yacht races are exciting.*

yawn (yawning, yawned)

to open your mouth and take a deep breath, usually when you are tired or bored *I can't stop yawning – I'm going to bed.*

year

a period of time that is equal to 12 months, especially from January to December *We're moving to a new house early next year.*

A B C D E F G H I J K L M

yes
a word that is used to say that you want something, that you will do something, that you agree with something or that something is true *Yes, I'd love to come to the cinema with you this evening.*

yesterday
the day before today *I phoned you yesterday.*

yoga
exercises for your body and mind *Yoga can help the body stay fit and healthy.*

yoghurt (yogurt)
a food made from milk *I'd like a strawberry yoghurt.*

young
not old *You're too young to walk to school on your own.*

yo-yo
a toy that moves up and down on a string that you hold in your hand *This yo-yo glows in the dark.*

▶ yo-yo

zebra
a wild, black-and-white striped horse *Zebras live in Africa.*

zero
nothing, 0 *The temperature is zero degrees.*

zip
a fastener made of two rows of teeth that lock together *My zip has broke.*

zoo
a place where wild animals are kept so that people can look at them and study them *We went to the zoo.*

N O P Q R S T U V W X Y Z

Junior Thesaurus

Your thesaurus will help you to use new or different words. Each double page has a new keyword with a choice of related words called synonyms – these are words that have the same meaning as another word. Each synonym is explained and placed in an example sentence. You will also find opposites, cartoons, games and fact panels. So brighten your emails, boost your vocabulary, but most of all, have fun with words!

Keyword and synonyms

Each keyword is in large type, and is followed by a line of synonyms. Each synonym is in alphabetical order.

Laugh
burst out laughing • cackle • chortle

• to laugh in a loud way

chuckle
to laugh quietly or to yourself
I could just hear my grandad chuckling.

The opposite of laugh is cry.

▶ roar with laughter

giggle
to laugh in a silly, quiet way because something is funny or you are embarrassed
We couldn't stop giggling at our teacher's tie.

• to laugh in a loud way because something is funny

burst out laughing
to laugh loudly and suddenly
We looked at her and burst out laughing.

guffaw
to laugh loudly in a way that is hard to control
We guffawed when she told us the joke.

roar with laughter
to laugh noisily and hard
The children roared with laughter.

A B C D E F G H I J K L

Opposites

There are small chalkboard panels throughout your book. These give the opposites of the keywords.

Alphabetical order

The words in this book are in alphabetical order. The coloured band along the bottom of every page will tell you which letter of the alphabet you are looking at.

Cartoons

These illustrate many of the words in your book in a fun way. Each cartoon has its own label to tell you exactly what it is.

Word partners

These are words that are often used together. Each word partner has an explanation and example sentence. Look for the pin boards!

Entries

Each synonym is explained and placed in an example sentence to show you how it could be used.

chuckle • giggle • guffaw • roar with laughter
snigger • titter

Word partners

hearty laughter
enthusiastic, happy laughter

hollow laughter
laughter without feeling

snigger/titter
to laugh at someone in an unkind way
Stop sniggering behind my back!
Let's see if you can do any better!

In other words

to be in stitches (idiom)
to be laughing so hard that you can't stop
The jokes had us in stitches.

. to laugh in an unpleasant way

cackle
to laugh loudly in a high voice
The witch cackled as she stirred the magic potion.

chortle
to laugh in a satisfied way, usually at or about someone else
They chortled as they played their trick.

N O P Q R S T U V W X Y Z

Did you know?

These panels give interesting information about words such as where they came from and how old they are.

Look for the green picture frames to have some fun! You can play games, solve puzzles and take part in quizzes.

In other words

An idiom is a phrasing of words that gives a different meaning from each of the words on their own. Idioms are fun ways to say things. We use them more in speech than when we are writing. Look for the speech bubbles to find more idioms.

Angry

annoyed • cross • furious • indignant

• feeling a little angry

annoyed
feeling slightly angry or impatient
Arran will be annoyed if we forget his birthday.

cross
feeling a little angry
Our teacher gets cross when we are naughty.

irritated
feeling annoyed about something that keeps happening
I'm really irritated – this game keeps crashing.

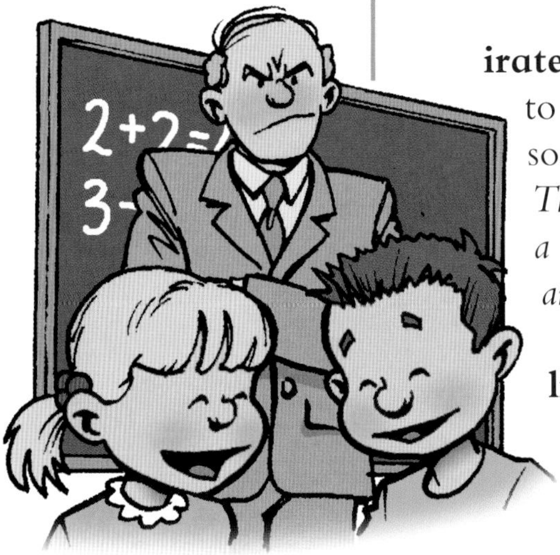

▲ cross

• feeling angry or very angry

furious
extremely angry
There was a furious row going on between the two teams.

irate
to feel angry because something has upset you
The Internet company received a lot of irate emails from angry customers.

livid
to feel so angry that you can't think
Angry? She was livid!

mad
feeling angry
This DVD player makes me so mad!

Put these words in order, from very angry to just a little bit angry:
a. annoyed b. furious
c. mad

Answers: b c a

resentful
feeling angry about something that is unfair and you cannot change
Some of us resent the new rules, but we all have to follow them.

seething
to be angry without saying a word
He was so tense, you could tell he was seething.

• feeling upset because something is wrong or not fair

indignant
feeling angry because something is wrong, unfair or insulting
Many parents wrote indignant letters when the playgroup closed.

In other words

to have steam coming out of your ears (idiom)
to be really angry about something
Wow! You could almost see the steam coming out of his ears!

N O P Q R S T U V W X Y Z

Argue

bicker • clash • debate • dispute • feud

• **to argue**

bicker
an argument that isn't too serious
They bickered about who should have won the game.

clash
to fight or argue in public
The rioters clashed with police.

fight/row ▼ squabble
to argue noisily
Why are you always fighting with your brother?

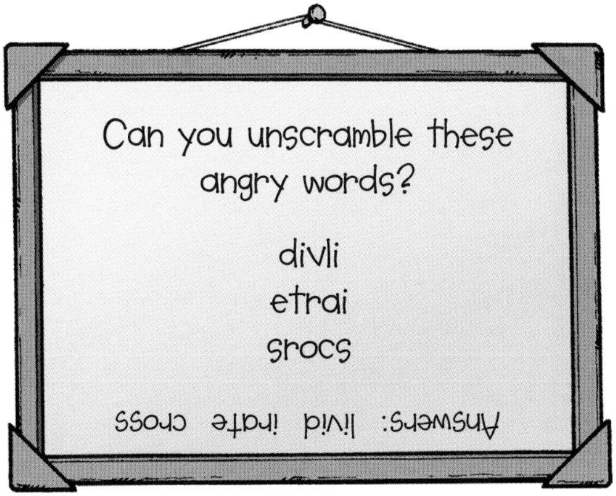

Can you unscramble these angry words?
divli
etrai
srocs
Answers: livid irate cross

quarrel
to argue with a friend or someone in your family
They quarrelled over whose turn it was to play the game.

squabble
to argue about something trivial.
Stop squabbling over those sweets!

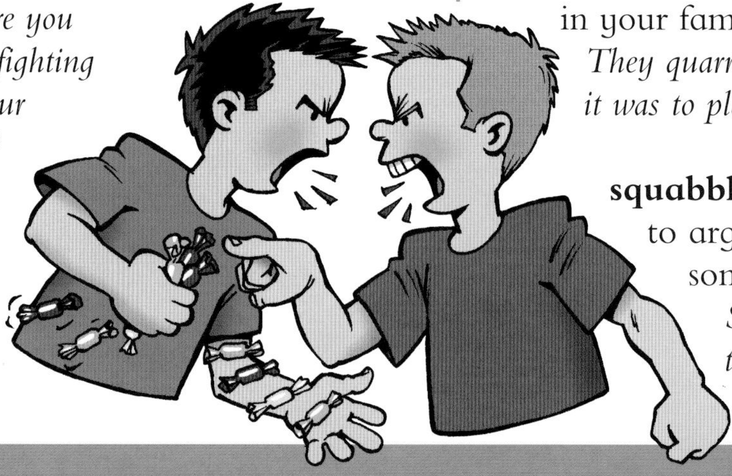

• **an argument**

debate
an argument where opposite views
are discussed
The debate was very heated.

dispute
an official fight between groups
or countries
The dispute was about land.

feud
a long fight between two groups
or families
Why did the family feud start?

The opposite of
angry is calm.

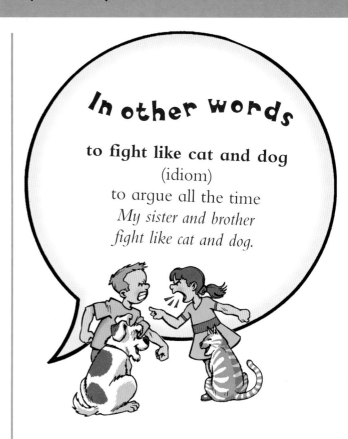

In other words

to fight like cat and dog
(idiom)
to argue all the time
*My sister and brother
fight like cat and dog.*

spat/tiff
a small argument
It was just a tiff – it will soon blow over.

Ask

consult • enquire • interrogate • interview

consult
to ask for advice or information from an expert
Consult your doctor first.

enquire
to ask for information
Tourists can enquire at the information centre.

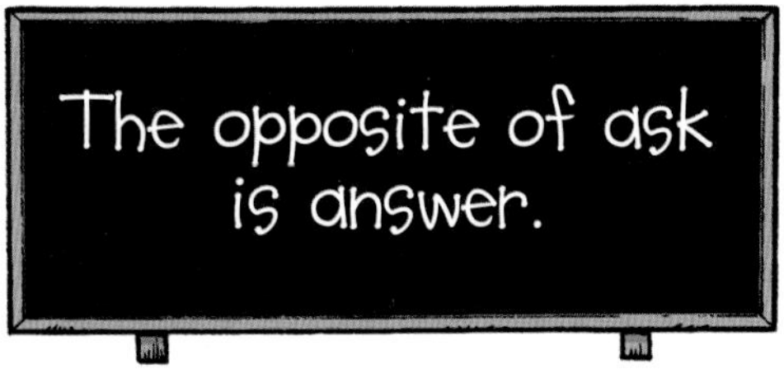

The opposite of ask is answer.

interrogate
to ask someone a lot of questions about a crime
The police interrogated the suspect for several hours.

interview
to ask someone questions for a newspaper or TV programme, or to find out if they are right for a job
The manager interviewed everyone who applied for the job.

plead
to ask someone for something that you really want
The children pleaded with their mother for some more chocolate.

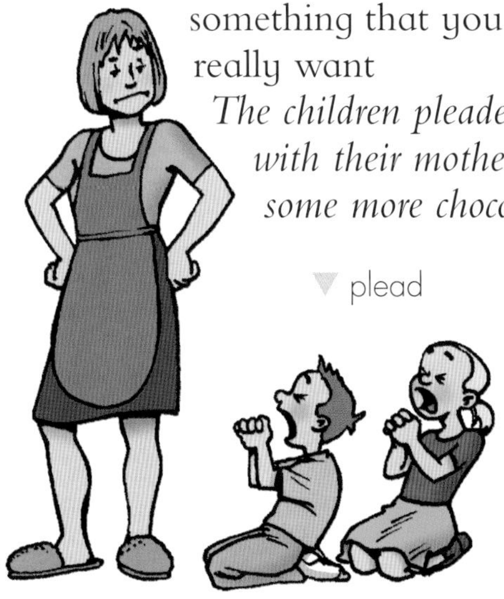

▼ plead

poll

a study that asks a lot of people about their opinion of something
The poll shows 75 percent of people agree with the laws.

pump

to ask someone a lot of questions to get as much information as possible
We pumped them for all the information about the new campsite.

query

to ask because you have not understood something or do not think it is right
They queried the bill.

question

to ask someone a lot of questions
The headmaster questioned each pupil about who had broken the window.

In other words

a loaded question (idiom)
a question that is asked in a certain way to get a certain answer
That's not fair – that's a loaded question!

quiz

to ask questions about something, usually in an annoying way
They quizzed us about the new teacher.

survey

to ask people a set of questions
We surveyed the school and found that most children have a mobile phone.

Bad

• **something that is bad**

appalling
something that seems bad in a shocking way
The prisoners' quarters were appalling.

dreadful
something that is very unpleasant or of poor quality
It was a dreadful film – don't bother to go and see it.

ghastly
something that is very unpleasant or shocking
That's a violent, ghastly game!

terrible
something that is very unpleasant or frightening
It was a terrible storm.

• **bad at doing something**

inept
not skilled
The inept goalkeeper let in a total of six goals.

In other words

to have a bad hair day (idiom)
a funny way to say that your hair is in a mess and everything is going wrong
I'm having a really bad hair day!

A B C D E F G H I K L M

> The opposite of bad is good.

hopeless/useless
to be not very good at doing something
I'm useless at maths, I can't even do simple sums.

• something that is not good quality

inferior
not as good as something or someone else
These trainers are cheaper than the more expensive brands but they're of inferior quality.

• badly behaved

mischievious
someone who causes minor annoyance or trouble
He had a very mischievious sense of humour.

naughty
badly behaved, usually to do with a child
It's very naughty to hit someone.

Did you know?
The great scientist Albert Einstein was useless at maths when he was young.

Call

- to say something loudly

cry
to speak in a loud voice because
something is wrong
"Get a doctor!" they cried.

scream
to cry out loudly because you are
excited, frightened or angry
*The witch turned and
all the children in
the audience
screamed
out loud.*

◀ scream

In other words

to call a spade a spade (idiom)
to tell the truth about
something, even if it is not
very polite
*She is very direct and just calls
a spade a spade.*

A B C D E F G H I J K L M

shout
to speak as loud as you can
No need to shout! I can hear you!

shriek
to give a short, high cry
We all shrieked and clapped when our team won the game.

yell
to speak in a loud voice, usually because you are angry
The prisoner was yelling at the policemen outside.

• **to order someone to come to a place**

summon
to order someone to be at a certain place
I was summoned to give evidence.

• **to telephone**

phone/ring
to telephone
I'll give you a ring later.

• **to call someone or something a name**

name
to give someone a name
What are you going to name the kitten?

Can you understand this text message?

Call me L8R-K8

Answer: Call me later – Kate

bring

to take something to the person speaking

Bring your homework to my house and we'll work on the essay together.

fetch

to go somewhere to get something and then bring it back

Our dog is good at fetching sticks.

haul

to drag or pull something heavy

Four men hauled the box around the corner.

▶ haul

▼ fetch

lift

to raise something in the air

We lifted the baby out of his pram.

lug

to carry something, especially something heavy

We lugged a big bag of newspapers around all the houses.

support
to hold something up
They supported the stone blocks on wooden logs and rolled them along.

take
to carry something in a direction away from the person speaking
Take your jacket with you, it's going to rain.

tote
to carry something, especially something awkward or large
You can take it, but you'll have to tote it around all day.

transport
to take goods from one place to another
Brand new cars are usually transported on special lorries.

In other words

to carry the weight of the world on your shoulders
(idiom)
to feel worried or sad about things
She looks so worried – as if she has the weight of the world on her shoulders.

Clever

brainy • bright • cunning • intellectual

· good at learning or thinking

brainy
intelligent and good at studying
Our last teacher liked brainy kids who got all the answers right.

bright
used to talk about someone who is intelligent and clever
George is one of the brightest pupils.

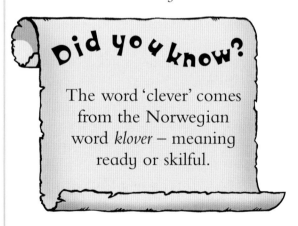

▲ bright

intelligent
good at learning and understanding things
You need to be intelligent to be a doctor.

quick
able to understand things quickly
She has a quick mind.

smart
someone who is able to solve problems or who learns easily
That's a great idea! You're so smart!

· having a lot of knowledge or information

intellectual
educated in subjects that need to be studied for a long time
The discussion was very intellectual.

Did you know?

The word 'clever' comes from the Norwegian word *klover* – meaning ready or skilful.

The opposites of clever are foolish and unintelligent.

streetwise
experienced in living in a city
The kids in that neighbourhood are pretty streetwise.

knowledgeable
knowing a lot about a subject
The librarian is knowledgeable about a lot of things.

• **good at using your brain to get along**

cunning
able to think and plan secretly so that you get what you want
They had a very cunning plan that almost worked.

In other words

a brain box (idiom)
someone who is very intelligent
She's a bit of a brain box – she won the school quiz.

Cold

• **something that is a bit cold**

chilly
quite cold
Autumn is here and it's starting to get chilly at night.

cool
slightly cold
There's a nice, cool breeze down on the beach.

In other words

cool as a cucumber (idiom)
very relaxed under pressure
Dom is always as cool as a cucumber during exam time.

draughty
a draughty place has cold air blowing through it
My room is cold and draughty.

◀ draughty

• something that is very cold

freezing
below the temperature at which
water freezes
Polar bears live in freezing conditions.

The opposite of
cold is hot.

frosty
extremely cold
It was a clear, frosty morning.

• a person or animal that is cold

shivering
to be so cold that you shake slightly
The puppies were wet and shivering.

to have goosepimples or goosebumps
to be so cold (or frightened) that
your skin raises up in little bumps
*By the end of the walk we were covered
in goosepimples.*

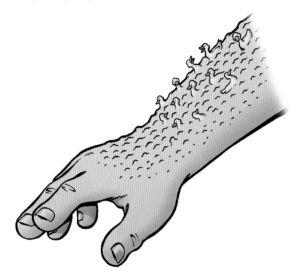

▲ goosepimples

Different

• unlike something else

dissimilar
not the same
The twins look dissimilar.

diverse
used to talk about many things being different from each other
The menu has very diverse dishes.

not at all like
something that is quite different
My house is not at all like yours.

• to be different from everything else

distinctive
something that is easy to recognise because it is different
The owl has a distinctive call.

individual
a different way of doing something
She has an individual way of singing.

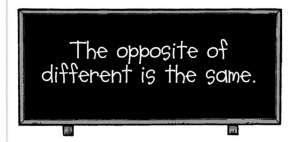

The opposite of different is the same.

unique
not like anything else
Seeing dolphins is a unique experience.

• to differ

contrast with
to be obviously different from something else
In contrast with the labrador, the Jack Russell is very lively.

A B C **D** E F G H I J K L M

vary
to be different from other things
in a group
*All the items of clothing vary in
size and colour.*

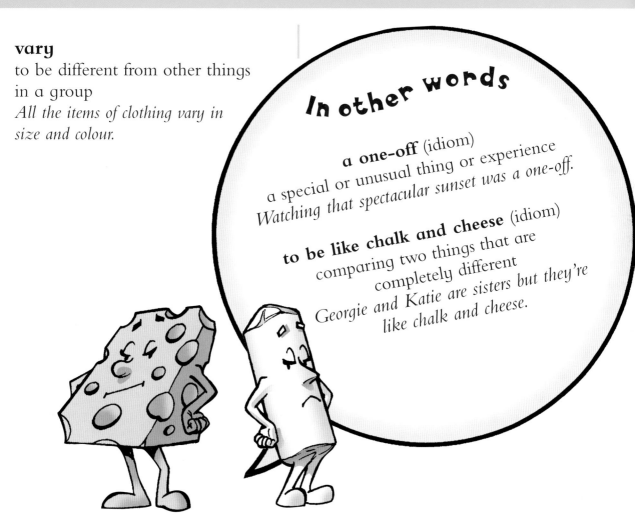

In other words

a one-off (idiom)
a special or unusual thing or experience
Watching that spectacular sunset was a one-off.

to be like chalk and cheese (idiom)
comparing two things that are
completely different
*Georgie and Katie are sisters but they're
like chalk and cheese.*

N O P Q R S T U V W X Y Z

Difficult

awkward • backbreaking • challenging

• not easy

awkward
difficult in a way that makes people uncomfortable
My little sister is always asking awkward questions.

challenging
something that is not easy but is interesting or fun to work on
Writing a page for our school website is challenging.

demanding
needing hard work or a big effort
Being at school all day can be demanding for young children.

hard
not easy to understand or do
These sums are really hard.

impossible
so difficult that it can't be done
It's impossible for me to meet you.

tough
needing a lot of thought or work
Those exams are very tough.

In other words

to make a meal of something
(idiom)
to pretend that a job is more difficult than it really is so that people will notice
Don't make such a meal of it, just do it!

A B C **D** E F G H I K L M

demanding • fiddly • gruelling • hard • impossible
strenuous • tough • tricky

• **not easy to do because it is complicated**

fiddly
full of lots of small things or problems
This jigsaw is really fiddly.

► tricky

tricky
full of problems
Decorating a birthday cake can be quite tricky.

gruelling
tiring and difficult because it lasts a long time
In Victorian times, children worked long, gruelling hours in factories.

strenuous
needing a lot of physical effort
Cross country skiing is a strenuous sport.

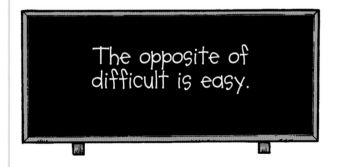

• **not easy to do because it is physically hard**

backbreaking
needing a lot of physical work, especially lifting heavy things
Gardening can be backbreaking work.

The opposite of difficult is easy.

N O P Q R S T U V W X Y Z

Drink

drain • gulp • guzzle • lap up

drain
to drink the last drop of something
Luke drained his water bottle before he got back to camp.

gulp
to drink something very quickly in large mouthfuls
I was so thirsty I gulped the juice down.

guzzle
to drink a lot of something very quickly
We guzzled our fizzy drinks.

lap up
the way animals drink with their tongues
The kittens lapped up all the milk.

Did you know?

The words 'lap', 'sip' and 'drink' all come from Old English.

polish off
to finish drinking something that you like
Hannah polished off all the apple juice.

 polish off

A B C **D** E F G H I J K L M

quench (your thirst)

to drink something so that you stop being thirsty

We stopped halfway up the hill and quenched our thirst.

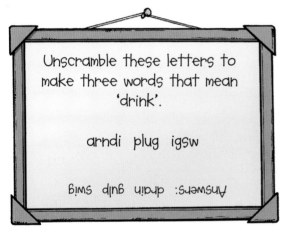

Unscramble these letters to make three words that mean 'drink'.

arndi   plug   igsw

Answers: drain gulp swig

swallow

to make something such as food or drink go down your throat

This milk tastes so sour that it's hard for me to swallow.

▶ swallow

sip

to drink small mouthfuls of something

Just sip water slowly after you've been running.

swig

to drink something in large mouthfuls

We walked around the funfair and swigged lemonade.

Easy

• **not difficult to understand or do**

effortless
something that is not easy, but it is made to look easy because someone does it well
Ballet dancers make dancing look so effortless.

simple
easy to do or understand
She knew the answers so the test was simple.

The opposite of easy is difficult.

In other words

a piece of cake (idiom)
something that is easy to do
That puzzle was a piece of cake!

straightforward
easy to do because it is clear what needs to be done
Painting walls is pretty straightforward.

uncomplicated
easy to understand or to do
Games for very young children need to be uncomplicated.

idiot-proof • painless • simple • straightforward uncomplicated • user-friendly

• easy to do

a breeze
very easy to do
The girls were much better so beating the boys was a breeze.

▶ a breeze

a doddle
very easy to do, especially things such as tests (informal)
The short words in the spelling test were a real doddle.

• easy to use

idiot-proof
extremely easy to use
You can buy digital cameras that are idiot-proof.

painless
not needing a lot of effort
Raising money for the school was painless.

user-friendly
clear and easy to use, especially to do with electronic things
This DVD is really user-friendly.

▶ user-friendly

N O P Q R S T U V W X Y Z

Eat

• **to eat food**

chew
to grind food with your teeth so
that you can swallow it
This meat is hard to chew.

consume
eat
*Once opened, this product should be
consumed within two days.*

feed
how animals eat
The panda feeds on bamboo.

▼ munch

munch
to eat noisily
*The people behind
us were munching
crisps all through
the film.*

• **to eat quickly**

bolt
to eat food quickly because you
are in a hurry
*We bolted our lunch so we could get
back to the game.*

demolish
a funny way to say that someone
ate all of something quickly
*They demolished the food at the party
within 15 minutes.*

devour
to eat something
quickly because
you are very
hungry
*We devoured the picnic
in minutes.*

A B C D E F G H I J K L M

• to eat a little

nibble
to take small bites
Our rabbit nibbles at carrots and lettuce.

▼ nibble

In other words

could eat a horse (idiom)
very hungry
What's for dinner? I could eat a horse!

gobble
to eat quickly
We gobbled our breakfast as we ran to catch the bus.

scoff
to eat something quickly and greedily
What! You scoffed the lot?

snack
a small meal or to eat a small meal
We had a snack when we got home because supper wasn't ready.

Fast

brisk
fast and energetic
We had a brisk walk along the seafront.

quick
fast
It was a quick decision.

rapid
very fast
The team made rapid progress.

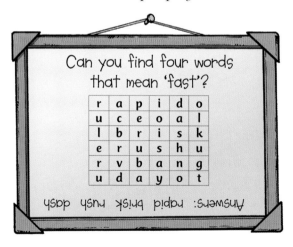

Can you find four words
that mean 'fast'?

r	a	p	i	d	o
u	c	e	o	a	l
l	b	r	i	s	k
e	r	u	s	h	u
r	v	b	a	n	g
u	d	a	y	o	t

Answers: rapid brisk rush dash

speedy
fast and successful
Wishing you a speedy recovery.

The opposite of
fast is slow.

• **moving fast**

quickly
fast, usually for a short time
Walk past the house as quickly.

• **to go fast**

accelerate
to go more quickly, usually in
a vehicle
The driver accelerated near the finish.

◁ dash

dash
to move quickly
They dashed out of the house to try and catch the bus.

rush
to move quickly because you are in a hurry
There's no need to rush your meal!

• capable of going fast

high-speed
to move very fast
The dentist uses a high-speed drill.

supersonic
can move faster than the speed of sound
Concorde *was a supersonic plane.*

Friend

• **friend**

buddy (mate/pal)
friend
We're all very good mates.

companion
someone you spend a lot of time with
They are travelling companions.

• **a group of friends**

circle
the people you know
We have a big circle of friends.

crowd
a group of friends you go out and do things with
A crowd of us are going out tonight, do you want to come?

In other words

china
mate
(Cockney rhyming slang)
This comes from 'china plate' which rhymes with mate.

gang
a group of friends that meet often
It's a nice gang of people.
• **friendly**

• friendly

amiable
friendly and likeable
He's so amiable and really easy to get along with.

hospitable
friendly and welcoming
Her parents are very hospitable and always ask us if we want something to eat or drink.

neighbourly
friendly and helpful
The new people next door are very neighbourly.

smarmy
someone who is polite and friendly but in a false way
I don't like him, he's smarmy.

sociable
friendly and out-going
Their family is very sociable, they have lots of parties.

warm
friendly and caring
Jemma is a sweet, warm girl.

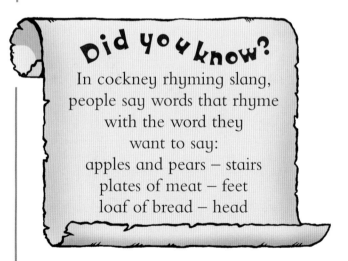

Did you know?
In cockney rhyming slang, people say words that rhyme with the word they want to say:
apples and pears – stairs
plates of meat – feet
loaf of bread – head

Frightened

afraid • chilling • dreading

• frightened

afraid
feeling nervous or
frightened of
something
*Are you afraid
of spiders?*

dreading
not wanting to do
something because
something bad may
happen
*I'm really dreading the
school play.*

panic-stricken
so frightened that you
can't think
*The panic-stricken people
tried to run away.*

petrified
to feel so frightened that you can't
even move
We were absolutely petrified.

scared
feeling worried that
something bad will
happen
*We were so scared, we
thought that someone
was trying to break
into the house.*

terrified
very frightened of something
dangerous or nasty
*They were terrified of the dog and just
ran without looking back.*

▲ afraid

A B C D E F G H I J K L M

• frightening

chilling
very frightening, sometimes in a
cruel or dangerous way
It was a chilling thought.

hair-raising
frightening because
something is
dangerous
*The story of their
escape was hair-raising.*

▶ hair-raising

In other words

**scared of your own
shadow** (idiom)
always nervous
and frightened
*He's scared of his own
shadow.*

scary
frightening
*That Hallowe'en mask is
too scary.*

spooky
frightening in a strange way
*The castle is really spooky in the
middle of the night.*

Funny

amusing • clown • comedian • comical

• making you laugh

amusing
funny and entertaining
Her stories are always amusing.

comical
funny in an unexpected way
Watching you try to catch the dog was really comical.

▼ comical

hilarious
extremely funny
The jokes on that website are hilarious.

humorous
funny, entertaining and clever
This is a humorous book about a trip around the world.

light-hearted
funny or poking fun in a gentle way
The programme is a light-hearted look at living on a farm.

In other words

a good sense of humour
an ability to laugh and see the funny side of things
He's got a good sense of humour and is a lot of fun to be with.

A B C D E F G H I J K L M

witty
using words in a funny and
entertaining way
Uncle Derek is very witty.

• **a person who is funny**

clown
a person whose
job it is to act
silly and make
people laugh
*The clown at
the circus had
us all in
stitches.*

How many words can you
make from 'hilarious'?
You should be able to
make at least six.

Answers: hi our sir so as sour

comedian
a person whose job is to
make people laugh
*I want to be a comedian
when I grow up.*

◀ clown

Give

• **to give something to someone**

donate
to give something to an organization or group
We donated a computer to charity.

hand
to pass something from your hand to another person's hand
Hand me that book, will you?

pass on
to give someone information or papers
Thanks, I'll pass it on to the manager.

The opposite of give is take.

slip
to give someone something secretly
She slipped me a note as I walked past.

◀ slip

• **to give someone something because of what they've done**

award
to officially give someone a prize
They awarded the medals after the competition.

present
to give someone something as part of a ceremony
The headmaster presented the prizes.

reward
to give someone something for being helpful
We rewarded the person who found our cat.

In other words

give and take (idiom)
a situation between two groups or two people when each is allowed some of the things they want
Brothers and sisters have to give and take.

• **to give something to a group**

distribute
to give something to a large group
The charity distributes medicine.

share out
to divide something into equal parts and give a part to each person in a group
We won a bag of sweets and shared them out among the team.

• **to arrange to give someone something after you die**

bequeath
to officially arrange to give someone something after you have died
They bequeathed the land to the tennis club.

Good

• **something you like or enjoy**

amazing/incredible
something that is good in a surprising way
This DVD is amazing!

brilliant
very, very good
This website is brilliant!

In other words
as good as gold
(idiom)
well behaved
Eliza has been as good as gold today.

excellent
extremely good
Their new CD is excellent.

fantastic/marvellous/wonderful
something good that makes you feel excited
The view from the top of the mountain is fantastic.

fun
enjoyable
This party game is fun.

great
very good or enjoyable
That ride is great! Let's go on it again.

lovely/nice
pleasant
Thank you for letting us stay, we've had a really nice time.

fantastic • fun • great • impressive • incredible • lovely
marvellous • nice • outstanding • talented • wonderful

• something that is very well done or of high quality

impressive ▼ outstanding
something that is done to a high standard that you admire
That last goal was really impressive.

outstanding
something that is noticeably better than others
Einstein was an outstanding scientist.

The opposite of good is bad.

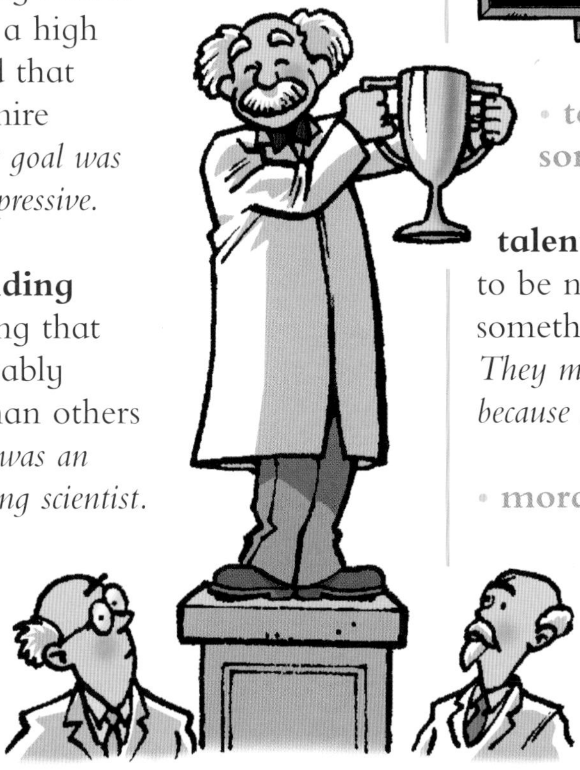

• to be able to do something well

talented
to be naturally able to do something well
They made him captain of the team because he is the most talented player.

• morally good

decent
good and honest
Giving the money to charity was the decent thing to do.

- **feeling happy**

cheerful
feeling happy most of the time
She's usually such a cheerful person to have around.

content
happy and satisfied in a quiet way
On a rainy day, I'm content sitting inside with a good book.

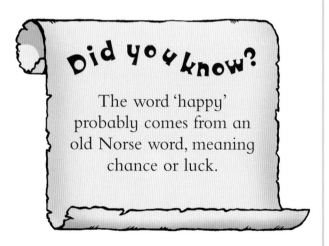

Did you know?

The word 'happy' probably comes from an old Norse word, meaning chance or luck.

jolly
happy or enjoyable
Old King Cole was a jolly old soul.

- **happy that something has happened**

delighted
very happy that something has happened
We're delighted to have won first place.

ecstatic
extremely happy and very excited that something has happened
The band was ecstatic when they won the music award.

glad
happy that something has happened or changed
I'm so glad I found my mobile phone.

ecstatic • glad • jolly • joyful
overjoyed • pleased • thrilled

In other words

over the moon (idiom)
very pleased about something
Mum got the job and she's over the moon.

overjoyed
very happy about some good news
They were overjoyed when they heard the results.

pleased
happy and satisfied that something good has happened
Our teachers were pleased with the art exhibition.

thrilled
very excited and happy
She was thrilled with the presents.

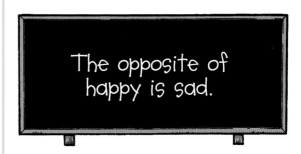

The opposite of happy is sad.

joyful
full of joy and happiness
The children were joyful that Christmas had arrived.

N O P Q R S T U V W X Y Z

• to dislike or hate something

abhor
to strongly dislike or disapprove of something
They abhor violence.

despise
to strongly dislike something and think it is wrong
We despise bullying.

detest
to strongly dislike or hate something or someone
Unfairness is something that most people detest.

▼ can't bear

loathe
to strongly dislike something
Some people loathe cabbage.

can't bear/stand
to dislike something so much that it upsets you
I can't bear scary movies!

▶ loathe

• a feeling of hating something or someone

animosity
a feeling of angry hatred
There is a great deal of animosity between the two teams.

contempt
a feeling of hatred about something that you think is worthless
The school has nothing but contempt for students who are bullies.

The opposite of hate is love.

In other words

a pet hate (idiom)
something that you don't like at all because it annoys you
Mobile phones are my teacher's pet hate.

N O P Q R S T U V W X Y Z

Hot

• **not cold**

lukewarm
only slightly warm (liquid or food)
The bathwater isn't really hot, just lukewarm.

scalding
very hot (liquid or steam)
Careful, that water is scalding!

warm
a temperature between hot and cool
Are you warm enough?

The opposite of hot is cold.

In other words

hot air (idiom)
when someone is full of hot air, they say things that they don't mean or don't really know
Their promises turned out to be so much hot air.

• **hot (weather or places)**

baking
very hot and dry
It's baking on the beach.

balmy
pleasantly warm
The weather is surprisingly balmy for the time of year.

boiling
very hot and uncomfortable
It's boiling in here, open a window.

muggy
hot and damp
Muggy weather makes you feel tired.

roasting
very hot and uncomfortable
I'm roasting in this sleeping bag.

▼ roasting

▲ sweltering

sweltering
very hot and damp
Sports day was unbearable – the weather was sweltering.

• **hot (food)**
spicy
tasting hot
Do you like very spicy curry?

conceive of

to invent something, like a plan or
an idea
*He conceived of the idea when he was
very young.*

daydream

to spend time imagining nice things
so that you forget about what you
are doing or where you are
Stop daydreaming and pay attention!

Word partners

a vivid imagination
a powerful ability to
imagine things
*My older sister has a very
vivid imagination.*

dream of

to imagine something good that
you want to happen
She's always dreamed of having a horse.

▶ fantasise

fantasise

to imagine something that probably
won't happen
*Mum and Dad fantasise about what
they'll do when they win the lottery.*

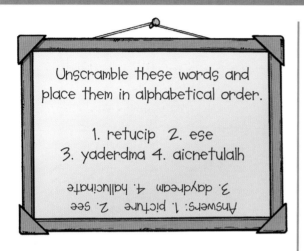

Unscramble these words and place them in alphabetical order.

1. retucip 2. ese
3. yaderdma 4. aicnetulalh

Answers: 1. picture 2. see
3. daydream 4. hallucinate

hallucinate
to believe that you can see things that aren't really there
Sometimes when you have a high fever, you hallucinate.

picture
to have a picture of something in your mind
I know who you mean but I can't picture his face.

see
to have a picture of something in your mind
I can just see you in that jacket.

visualise
to get a clear picture of something in your mind
I'm sorry, I can't visualise what you mean.

picture

Important

central
main
Peter Pan is the central character in the play.

▼ central

critical
extremely important to the success of something
Finishing on time is critical.

crucial
important because other things depend on it
The support of parents is crucial.

essential
important to the highest degree
It is essential that we leave work on time this evening.

historic
so important that it will cause something to be remembered as part of history
It was a historic decision.

key
important to what will happen
Hard work is a key factor to the success of the company.

The opposite of important is unimportant.

essential • historic • key • major
notable • significant • vital • weighty

In other words

VIP (abbreviation)
Very Important Person
They treated us like VIPs.

significant
having an important effect
It is a significant win.

vital
very important and
necessary
Your help is vital.

 weighty

major
one of the most important
Edinburgh is a major Scottish city.

notable
important and deserving attention
*A notable feature of the school is the
sports centre.*

weighty
important and
serious
*These are weighty
questions.*

N O P Q R S T U V W X Y Z

Job
assignment • chore • duty • errand • mission

assignment
a piece of work that
someone gives you
*The assignment
is to write a
600-word essay.*

▶ assignment

chore
a boring job you
have to do often
*Feeding the pets isn't really a chore,
it's fun.*

duty
something that you have a
responsibility to do
At scout camp, everyone has duties.

errand
a small job
*While you're out, will you run some
errands for me?*

mission
an important job that
someone goes
somewhere to do
*The mission is to bring
back the secret formula.*

project
an important piece
of work that needs lots of
planning
This is a long-term project.

task
a piece of work
*Each person is given a task so that the
work gets done more quickly.*

undertaking
a big and important job
*Raising money for a new sports hall is
a huge undertaking.*

A B C D E F G H I J K L M

• jobs that people do to earn money

occupation
a person's full-time job
His occupation is police officer.

profession
a job for which you need special training
He's a doctor by profession

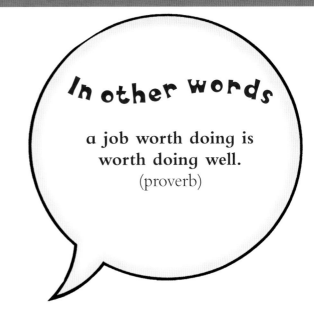

In other words

a job worth doing is worth doing well.
(proverb)

Unscramble the letters to find four words that mean 'job'.

1. ktsa   2. reoch
3. rrndea   4. uytd

Answers: 1. task 2. chore
3. errand 4. duty

trade
a skilled job that you use your hands to do
He chose carpentry as his trade.

vocation
a job that you do because you feel strongly about doing it
Teaching and nursing are vocations.

N O P Q R S T U V W X Y Z

Joke

▶ pun

gag
a short joke
The comedian had some good gags.

in jest
said to make people laugh
It was said in jest – he didn't really mean it!

practical joke
a carefully planned joke
My brother played a practical joke on his best friend.

prank
a silly trick that isn't supposed to hurt anyone
We played a few pranks on Hallowe'en.

pun
a play on words that sound the same but mean something else
a pun: Why was six scared of seven? Because seven eight nine!

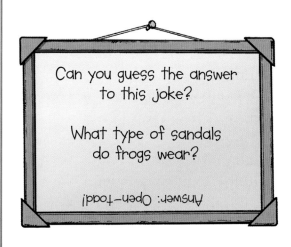

Can you guess the answer to this joke?

What type of sandals do frogs wear?

Answer: Open-toad!

to be joking/kidding
not serious
I was only joking, I didn't really forget your birthday!

wisecrack
a funny, clever remark
He's full of wisecracks!

▲ wisecrack

punch line
the last line of a joke that makes it funny
Mum loves to tell jokes but she always forgets the punch line.

riddle
a strange or difficult question that usually has a funny answer
Not all riddles are jokes.

In other words

to pull someone's leg (idiom)
to tell someone something that isn't true, as a joke
I think Joe was pulling your leg, there isn't a frog in the bath.

N O P Q R S T U V W X Y Z

Jump

bound • hop • hurdle • leap

bound
to move quickly with big jumps
Kangaroos bound across the bush.

hop
to jump on one leg
The first part of the race is hopping for 25 metres.

hurdle
to jump over something while you are running
They hurdled the fence.

leap
to jump a long way
It was a huge leap from one step to the next.

In other words

jump the gun (idiom)
do something too soon
Now, don't jump the gun. Let's just think about this a bit more.

jump to conclusions (idiom)
to decide what you think about something before you know all the facts
I'm not to blame! Why do you always jump to conclusions about me?

▲ pounce

pounce
to jump to catch something
The cat pounced on the mouse.

A B C D E F G H I J K L M

skip

to go forward with small, quick jumps

We tried to skip all the way to school but we got too tired.

▶ vault

vault

to jump over something

The thief vaulted over the wall.

▲ spring

spring

to jump suddenly and quickly

The cheetah seemed to spring from nowhere.

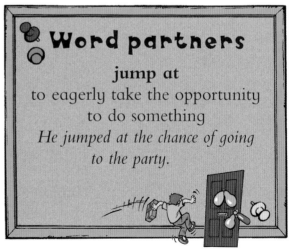

🔵 Word partners

jump at

to eagerly take the opportunity to do something

He jumped at the chance of going to the party.

N O P Q R S T U V W X Y Z

Know

appreciate • be aware of • be familiar with

• to know something

appreciate
to understand that a situation is difficult or important
Do you appreciate how serious this situation could be?

be aware of
to know about something
Are you aware of the new rule?

be familiar with
to know about something
We're familiar with the area, we went there on holiday last year.

be well-up on
to be well-informed and up to date about a subject
He's well-up on the dates of all the important football fixtures.

feel
to know something through your feelings
You could feel the tension in the room.

realise
to notice or understand something that you didn't before
I didn't realise it was so late.

▲ feel

sense
to have the strong feeling that you know something even though there is no proof
They sensed something was in the room.

• **a person who knows about something**

expert
someone who knows a lot about a certain subject
He's an expert cook.

specialist
someone who has studied a subject carefully and knows a lot about it
She's a specialist in Chinese medicine.

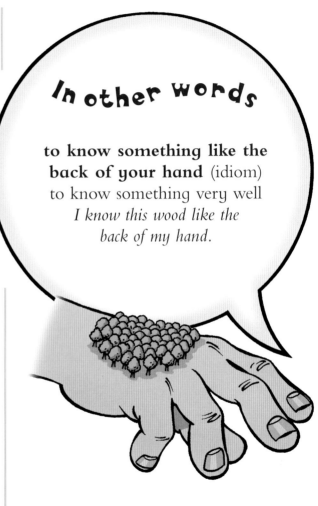

In other words

to know something like the back of your hand (idiom)
to know something very well
I know this wood like the back of my hand.

e	o	d	a	l
s	o	s	e	l
i	f	e	e	l
l	i	n	l	r
a	i	s	i	r
e	v	e	o	i
r	s	t	s	t

Can you find three words that mean 'know'?

Answers: realise feel sense

N O P Q R S T U V W X Y Z

• to laugh in a loud way

chuckle
to laugh quietly or to yourself
I could just hear my grandad chuckling.

The opposite of
laugh is cry.

▶ roar with laughter

giggle
to laugh in a silly,
quiet way because
something is funny or
you are embarrassed
*We couldn't stop giggling
at our teacher's tie.*

• to laugh in a loud way
because something is funny

burst out laughing
to laugh loudly and suddenly
We looked at her and burst out laughing.

guffaw
to laugh loudly in a way that is
hard to control
We guffawed when she told us the joke.

roar with laughter
to laugh noisily and hard
The children roared with laughter.

chuckle • giggle • guffaw • roar with laughter
snigger • titter

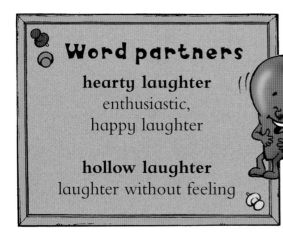

Word partners

hearty laughter
enthusiastic,
happy laughter

hollow laughter
laughter without feeling

snigger/titter
to laugh at someone in an
unkind way
Stop sniggering behind my back!
Let's see if you can do any better!

In other words

to be in stitches (idiom)
to be laughing so hard that
you can't stop
The jokes had us in stitches.

• to laugh in an unpleasant way

cackle
to laugh loudly in a high voice
*The witch cackled as she stirred the
magic potion.*

chortle
to laugh in a satisfied way, usually
at or about someone else
They chortled as they played their trick.

N O P Q R S T U V W X Y Z

Look

examine • gaze • glance • glare • glimpse

• to look at or see something quickly

glance
to look at something or someone for a short time
She glanced at her watch.

glimpse
to see someone or something for a very short time
We just glimpsed some baby birds.

• to notice or see something

▶ peep

spot
to see or notice something or someone
We spotted several people who were wearing the same costume.

spy
to see or notice something or someone, usually from a distance
We spied them coming up the street.

• to look at someone or something secretly

peek
to look at something quickly and secretly
They peeked at the presents under the Christmas tree.

peep
to look at something for a short time, usually when you don't want anyone to see you
Maddy peeped around the corner to see if her brothers were still waiting for her.

A B C D E F G H I J K L M

• **to look at something for a long time**

gaze
to look at someone or something for a long time, usually with a good feeling
We gazed up at the stars in the sky.

glare
to stare angrily at someone or something
They glared at each other.

◀ glare

stare
to look directly at someone or something without moving your eyes away
It's rude to stare.

• **to look at something or someone carefully**

examine
to look at something very carefully, usually to discover something
They examined the fossils closely.

inspect
to look at something carefully, to make sure it is safe or correct
They inspect all the tyres.

peer
to look carefully at something, because you can't see it very well
They peered into the cave.

study
to look at something carefully, to learn or understand something
Study the map closely.

Loud

• very loud

blaring
making a loud noise
The song starts with blaring horns and loud drums.

booming
very loud and deep
We could hear Joe's booming voice from outside.

deafening
so loud that you can't hear anything else
The explosion was deafening.

> The opposites of loud are soft and low.

thunderous
extremely loud
When the music stopped, the applause was thunderous.

• unpleasantly loud

ear-splitting
so loud that it hurts your ears
The fire alarm is ear-splitting.

▶ ear-splitting

noisy
loud in an unpleasant way
It's noisy in the swimming pool today.

A B C D E F G H I J K L M

In other words

Sometimes we use 'loud' to describe things such as clothes that are unpleasantly colourful.

Word partners

Loud and clear
something that is obvious and easy to understand
We understood the message loud and clear.

penetrating
loud, clear and unpleasant
The ship's horn gives a penetrating blast.

piercing
loud and high-pitched
She's got such a piercing voice, it went straight through me.

▲ piercing

rowdy
people who are noisy and quite badly behaved
A few of the team were rowdy last night.

N O P Q R S T U V W X Y Z

Love

• **to love someone**

be close to
to love someone you can talk to easily
I'm very close to my older sister.

be fond of
to like someone very much
They're very fond of each other.

care about
to feel concerned about and like someone
We care about all children, everywhere.

▶ be close to

• **to love someone or something very much**

adore
to really love someone or something
Molly adores chocolate.

▶ adore

be devoted to
to love and be loyal to someone
My grandparents are devoted to each other.

A B C D E F G H I J K L M

The opposite of love is hate.

worship
to love or admire someone or something very much
He worships the basketball team!

• feeling or showing love for someone or something

affectionate
showing love
Our baby brother is very affectionate.

doting
showing love by paying attention to someone
They are doting grandparents.

passionate
a very strong feeling of love or devotion
She felt passionately about saving endangered animals.

tender
gentle and loving
She gave the children a tender look as she tucked them into bed.

Word partners

fall in love
to become very fond of someone or something

love at first sight
to fall in love immediately

Make

assemble • build • concoct • create

assemble
to put together the parts of something
We have to assemble the desk from a kit.

build
to make something by putting parts together
They're building a clubhouse for kids only.

concoct
to make something strange to eat or drink
The wizard concocted a magic potion.

▶ concoct

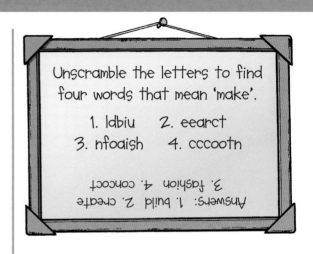

create
to make something that wasn't there before
Our class created a sculpture for the park.

fashion
to make something to do a particular job
The castaway fashioned a sail for the raft.

form
to make (or be a part of) something
*Water is formed from hydrogen
and oxygen.*

In other words

cobble something together
(idiom)
to make something roughly
and quickly
*We didn't have a real go-cart but we
cobbled something together.*

generate
to make something by using
a process
The power station generates electricity.

manufacture
to make something, especially in
a factory
They manufacture toys.

mould
to shape a substance, such as clay
or wax
Wax is moulded into candles.

produce
to make something
*Spring is the time when many plants
produce flowers.*

The opposite of
make is destroy.

Mistake

blunder • error • fault • gaffe

• a mistake

blunder
a stupid or clumsy mistake
It was a foolish blunder.

error
a serious mistake you don't know
you're making
*They made an error when they charged
us for the meal.*

fault
a mistake, usually that someone
or something is to blame for
*I think the entire system of filing
information is at fault.*

gaffe
an embarrassing mistake
*Putting sugar on your eggs in the
restaurant was a real gaffe.*

oversight
a mistake you make by forgetting
or not noticing something
*Everyone should have been invited –
leaving their names off was an oversight.*

▲ slip

slip
a small mistake that is easy
to correct
It was just a slip of the tongue.

In other words

put your foot in it (idiom)
to say something stupid
or secret that you shouldn't
have said
*You really put your foot in it when
you mentioned the surprise party!*

misjudge
to make a mistake by deciding
to do the wrong thing
They misjudged the situation.

mix-up
to make a mistake that
confuses things
*We were supposed to
play yesterday
but there was
a mix-up with
the dates.*

• **to make a mistake**

goof
to make a silly mistake
I goofed the answer.

cash
notes and coins used as money
Do you have any cash with you?

change
money that you get back when you pay for something
Make sure you check your change.

coins
small pieces of metal used as money
Some vending machines only take coins, not notes.

currency
the type of money that is used in a country
The dollar is the currency in Canada, the USA and Australia.

• **a lot of money**

a fortune
a very large amount of money
What a fantastic idea! We should be able to make a fortune.

In other words

money doesn't grow on trees (idiom)
often used if money is in short supply, or to explain that you should spend money wisely
No, you can't have a new bike — money doesn't grow on trees you know!

wealth
a large amount of money
The king had great wealth.

• **amounts of money**

figure
an exact amount of money
The figure we decided on is £34.98.

sum
an amount of money
It added up to a good sum.

• **money that someone gives to another person**

allowance
money someone receives regularly, not for working
The allowance from her parents covers basic living expenses.

income
money that people receive, usually from working
Our joint income means we can afford to go on holiday.

pocket money
money that children receive from their parents each week
I work for my dad on Saturdays to earn pocket money.

Did you know?

The word 'money' probably comes from Moneta, a name given to the Roman goddess Juno, whose temple was used to store valuable things.

Move

budge
to move a little way
This is stuck, it won't budge.

relocate
to move something permanently
to another place
*We're moving house – Dad's firm
has relocated to another city.*

shift
to move from one place to another
We shifted the sofa out of the way.

transfer
to move from one place to another
The player transferred to another team.

transport
to take people or goods from one
place to another
The new cars are transported by rail.

• **people or animals moving
their bodies**

squirm
to move your body from side to
side because you are uncomfortable
Stop squirming and sit still.

stir
to move sightly
*She stirred slightly in her sleep but
didn't wake up.*

◀ stir

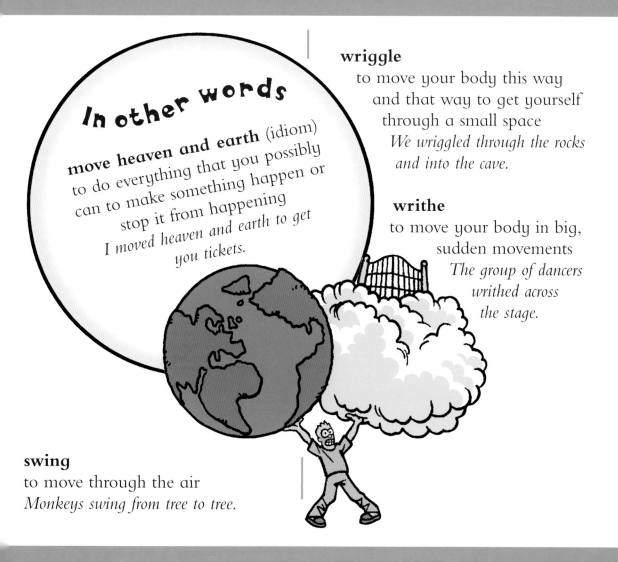

In other words

move heaven and earth (idiom)
to do everything that you possibly can to make something happen or stop it from happening
I moved heaven and earth to get you tickets.

wriggle
to move your body this way and that way to get yourself through a small space
We wriggled through the rocks and into the cave.

writhe
to move your body in big, sudden movements
The group of dancers writhed across the stage.

swing
to move through the air
Monkeys swing from tree to tree.

• people's names

identity

a person's name

The police are keeping his identity a secret.

initial

the first letter of each of your names

Her initials are BJH.

Did you know?

'Anonymous' is the name that people put at the end of poems, stories and plays when they don't want people to know who wrote them.

maiden name

a married woman's surname before she was married

These days, many women keep their maiden names after they get married.

▶ namesake

namesake

a person who has the same name as you, especially a famous person

Our dog's namesake is Beckham.

nickname
a name your friends or family call you
Her nickname is Bizzy.

• **false names**

alias
a different name someone is known by, especially a criminal
He was living here under an alias.

pen name
another name writers use instead of their own names
Mark Twain is the pen name of Samuel

Clemens.

pseudonym
a name used by someone instead of their real name
Singers and actors sometimes use pseudonyms.

• **names for things**

brand name
the name a company gives a product
Playstation® is a brand name.

code name
a secret name for someone or something
The army called the new project Operation Storm Cloud.

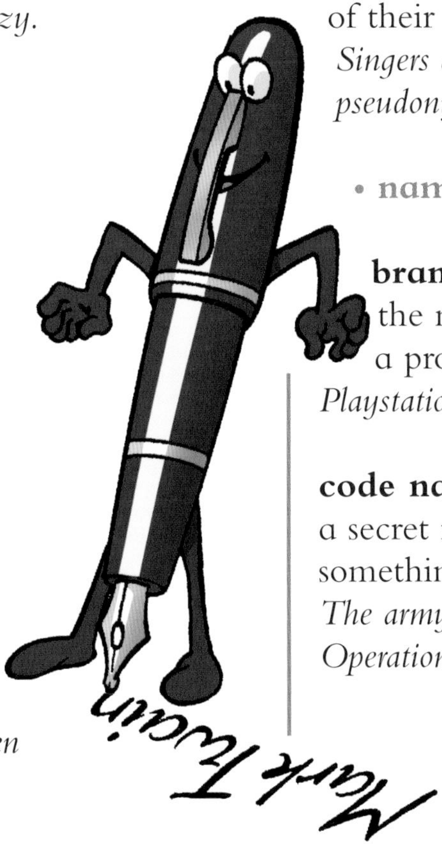

◀ pen name

Near

close • handy • in the vicinity • local • nearby

close
very near
The swimming pool is close to home.

handy
conveniently near
The shop is just around the corner from our house, which is handy.

in the vicinity
in the area around a place
Police believe the thief is still in the vicinity.

▲ in the vicinity

In other words

on your doorstep (idiom)
very near the place where you live
Sam likes living in a city because everything is on his doorstep.

local
near a place, in an area
Can you tell me where the local post office is?

nearby
near where you are
Is there a leisure centre nearby?

A B C D E F G H I J K L M

neighbouring
near the place where you live or the place you are talking about
The secondary school is in the neighbouring village.

The opposite of near is far.

next
the one that is closest
My best friend lives in the house next door.

surrounding
near and around a place
There are two supermarkets in the surrounding area.

within walking distance
close enough to walk to easily
We have a cinema within walking distance of our house.

◀ next

New

brand new • fresh • innovative • just out

brand new
completely new
We've just bought a brand new car.

just out
very new
Have you heard their latest album, it's just out on CD?

latest
the most recent
I've just bought the latest version of the game.

modern
up to date
The modern houses on the estate make ours seem very old-fashioned in comparison.

▲ brand new

fresh
clean, new and not used
The tennis players asked for fresh balls.

innovative
new, different and better
The skateboard is an innovative design.

The opposite of new is old.

novel
something that is new, interesting and different
Our teacher said having hot drinks at break was a novel idea.

In other words

hot off the press (idiom)
the latest news
This is the news from the Olympics — hot off the press.

original
new, not done before
He had original ideas about the building work.

pioneering
done for the first time
Marie Curie carried out pioneering research in the science world.

newcomer
a person who has recently arrived in a place
The family are newcomers to the town.

recent
something that was made or done a short time ago
We are looking for recent articles about the zoo.

N O P Q R S T U V W X Y Z

• things that are old

ancient
extremely old, existing many years ago
Archimedes was a scientist in ancient Greece.

▼ ancient

In other words

as old as the hills (idiom)
very old
That joke is as old as the hills!

antique
old and valuable
My grandfather gave me an antique pocket watch.

second-hand
owned by someone else before you
Charity shops sell second-hand clothes.

used
not new, or owned by someone else before
Used computers for sale are advertised in the local newspaper.

vintage
old and one of the best of its type
Vintage wine is very expensive.

• **people who are old**

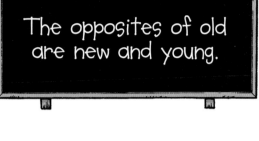

The opposites of old
are new and young.

ageing
becoming older
The UK has an ageing population.

to be getting on
getting older
Grandad is getting on a bit.

elderly
old
*Gran
is quite
elderly but
she still likes
to go cycling
with us.*

veteran
old and experienced
Dad plays on the veteran team.

• **things or places for people
who are old**

▲ elderly

geriatric
to do with old people
*Geriatrics is the branch of medicine
concerned with elderly people.*

force
to open something that is stuck or
locked by pushing hard on it
The firefighters forced the lift doors open.

pick a lock
to open a lock with something that
is not a key
*Car locks are extra safe so thieves can't
pick the locks.*

Word partners

an open mind
Not decided in
advance
*He kept an open
mind about the
holiday.*

◀ prise

prise
to force something apart to open it
The trunk was prised open.

unbolt
to open a door or gate by sliding
a metal bar across
*Carefully unbolt the door and lead
the pony out.*

unfold
to open paper or cloth and spread
it out
*Unfold the map and try to find out
where we are.*

unlock
to open a lock using a key
Can you unlock the door? My hands are full.

unwrap
to open a parcel by taking paper or cloth off it
We can't wait to unwrap our presents on Christmas morning.

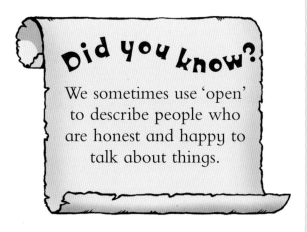

Did you know?
We sometimes use 'open' to describe people who are honest and happy to talk about things.

• **to be open**

ajar
slightly open
If the door is ajar, just go straight in.

wide open
completely open
We left the garage door wide open by mistake.

 ajar

unscrew
to take the top off a container by turning it
If you can't unscrew something, try using a cloth to hold it.

Ordinary

average • banal • bland • commonplace

average
typical, like most others of the same type
An average lesson lasts 45 minutes.

banal
ordinary, not interesting or new
Some people think the words in pop songs are banal.

bland
boring, dull or not tasty
Bland foods are not spicy.

commonplace
an everyday happening or sight
Red buses are commonplace in the city.

everyday
not unusual or special
The Internet is a part of everyday life now.

mundane
ordinary and dull
Cleaning the rabbit's cage is a mundane task.

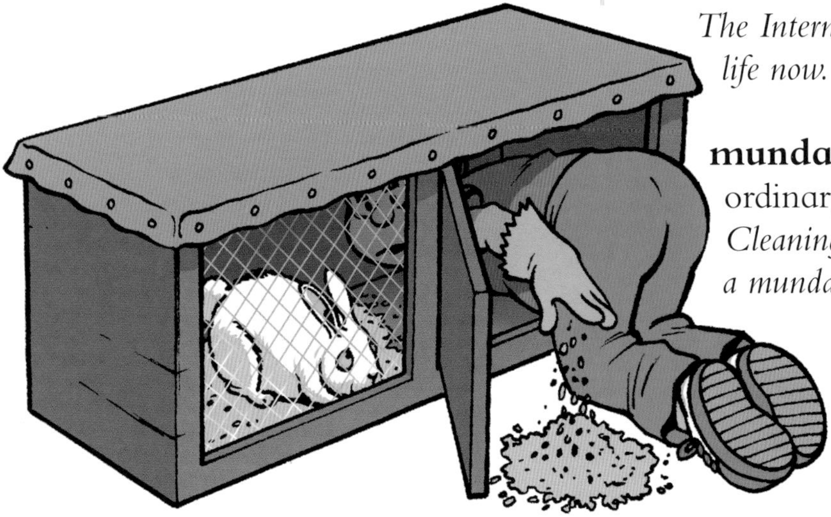

◀ mundane

neutral
plain, without strong colours, flavours or opinions
I've painted the entire house in neutral colours.

normal
like other people or things of the same type
His height and weight are normal for his age.

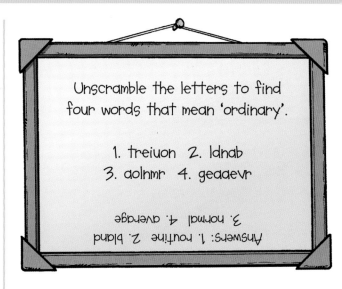

Unscramble the letters to find four words that mean 'ordinary'.

1. treiuon 2. ldnab
3. aolnmr 4. geaaevr

Answers: 1. routine 2. bland
3. normal 4. average

routine
usual and done frequently
It's just a routine dental check-up.

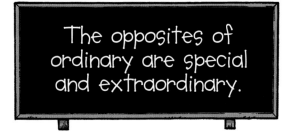

The opposites of ordinary are special and extraordinary.

standard
something basic without extra features
The company has a standard document for sending emails.

typical
usual
They really are just a typical family trying to make ends meet.

bit
a small part
Would you like to taste a bit of this chocolate bar?

branch
an office or shop that is part of a big organisation
Mum works in the local branch of the bank.

component
part of a machine or system
The hard disk is a component of computers.

cross-section
a part of something that is cut or divided to show how the rest works or looks
This cross-section shows the different layers of skin.

crumb
a small bit of bread or cake
Who ate all the cake? There are only crumbs left!

▲ crumb

element
one of the separate parts of something
Different levels are an important element of any good computer game.

fraction
a small part of an amount or number
We've only raised a fraction of the amount we need.

ingredient
part of a food recipe
Mix all the ingredients together.

The opposites of part are whole and all.

In other words

part and parcel (idiom)
a necessary part of something
Homework is part and parcel of being at school.

portion
part of something larger
A portion of the profit goes to charity.

section
a part of something that is separate from something else
Which section of the school is your classroom in?

segment
a part of something such as fruit
Divide the orange into segments before you put it in the fruit salad.

Payment

• payment for work or service

bonus
extra money for working hard
Dad got a bonus for getting a new account.

fee
the amount of money paid for something
The school fees are high.

salary
the total payment someone gets each year for doing a job
Mum's salary is higher now that she has a new job.

wages
the money that someone gets each week for doing a job
Wages are paid every Thursday.

• payment in a restaurant

tip
money that you give a waiter for service
Are you going to leave a tip?

▲ tip

• payment as a punishment

fine
money paid for breaking the law
We had to pay a parking fine.

• payment to get something

bribe
payment to a person so that they will do something, usually against the law
The prisoner bribed the guard to let him out of his cell.

deposit
a payment you make when you decide to buy something, to prove that you will buy it
I've paid a £10 deposit on the CD player I want.

instalment
a partial payment that you make to buy something over a period of time
I paid for the holiday in six monthly instalments.

In other words

pay through the nose
(idiom)
pay too much for something
You have to pay through the nose for some trainers.

refund
money that you get back when you return something, usually to a shop
We got a full refund on the television.

Person

family

a group of people who are related

How many kids are there in your family?

▼ family

folk

people

They're friendly folk.

humanity

all the people who have ever lived

Cave paintings are early records of humanity.

humankind

all the people in the world

This is something for all humankind to be proud of.

individual

one person

Every classroom is made up of unique individuals.

human/human being

a man, woman or child

The gorillas are not used to seeing humans.

kin

members of a family

Next of kin means the person you are most closely related to.

A B C D E F G H I J K L M

Unscramble the letters to find
four family members.

1. ousinc 2. ceine
3. uelnc 4. nweehp

Answers: 1. cousin 2. neice
3. uncle 4. nephew

hero/heroine
the main character in a story, or a
person who does something brave
The hero killed the dragon.

somebody/someone
a person – used when you do not
know the person's name or when it
is not important to use their name
Quick, somebody call an ambulance!

• **people in a story**

character
a person who appears in a book,
film, game or story
Who is your favourite character?

In other words

person in the street (idiom)
ordinary people
We say 'the man or woman in the
street' to talk about what most people
think. Sometimes we
say 'Joe Public' to talk
about the average
person.

Poor

broke • deprived • destitute • disadvantaged

broke
not having any money temporarily
I can't come out tonight, I'm broke until Friday.

deprived
not having the things you need for a normal life
Charles Dickens had a deprived childhood.

The opposite of poor is rich.

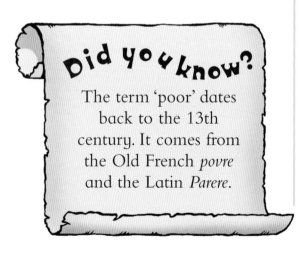

Did you know?
The term 'poor' dates back to the 13th century. It comes from the Old French *povre* and the Latin *Parere*.

destitute
so poor that you do not have basic things such as enough food
The refugees are destitute.

disadvantaged
not having the same opportunities as other people
The charity helps disadvantaged families.

impoverished
made poor
The country was impoverished after many years of drought.

A B C D E F G H I J K L M

needy
not having enough money
Anyone who is needy is welcome to come for a free meal.

underprivileged
poor and with fewer opportunities than other people
We collect aluminium cans to raise money for underprivileged families.

▲ penniless

penniless
without any money
The winning lottery ticket was found by a penniless beggar.

In other words

as poor as church mice (idiom)
very poor
My grandparents were as poor as church mice when they first came to this country.

Pretend

• to pretend

bluff
to pretend that you will do
something or that you know
something
*Do you really know the answer or are
you just bluffing?*

impersonate
to pretend you are someone else
*He was arrested for impersonating
a policeman.*

masquerade
to dress up in a disguise
They masqueraded as children.

pose as
to pretend to be someone else
*She was posing as the head of the
committee.*

• not real

artificial
not real or not natural
The coats were made with artificial fur.

fake/false
something that pretends to look
similar to something else
Are you wearing false eyelashes?

▼ false

impersonate • impostor • insincere
make-believe • masquerade • pose as

In other words

to cry crocodile tears
(idiom)
to pretend to be upset
Your crocodile tears don't fool me.

make-believe
not real
The film is just make-believe.

• **people who pretend**

impostor
a person who pretends to be someone else
The king was really an impostor.

Did you know?

In England in 1491, Perkin Warbeck pretended to be one of the Princes in the Tower, who had supposedly been murdered by their uncle, Richard III.

insincere
not really meaning what you say
His apology sounded very insincere

N O P Q R S T U V W X Y Z

Problem

catch
a hidden problem
There is a catch for arriving so late: you have to work through your lunch hour today.

complication
a problem that makes a situation more difficult
I will be on time unless there are complications.

difficulty
a problem that is not easy to deal with
I'm having difficulty choosing which car to buy.

dilemma
a very difficult choice
We have a major dilemma — we can go out, but we have to take my little brother with us.

In other words

stumbling block (idiom)
a problem that is likely to stop someone from doing what they want to do
Time may be the stumbling block.

hassle

an annoying problem
We had a bit of hassle getting the dog into the car.

▶ hassle

hiccup

a small problem that is quickly solved
There was a minor hiccup but nothing serious to worry about.

hindrance

something that stops you from doing something easily
I was trying to wash our car but the rain was a real hindrance.

hurdle

a problem that you have to solve so that you can do what you are trying to do
The team has had to overcome several hurdles: injuries, player moves and lack of funds.

snag

a difficulty
The snag is, tickets are very expensive.

▼ hindrance

Promise

assure • deliver • give your word

• to make a promise

assure
to say that something is true or that
something will happen to make
someone feel better
The vet assured us nothing was wrong.

give your word (of honour)
to make a very serious promise
He gave his word that he would return.

guarantee
to say that something is true or that
something will happen because you
are very sure about it
I guarantee there won't be any problems.

pledge
to say that you will do something
or give something
We pledged £5 for the sponsored walk.

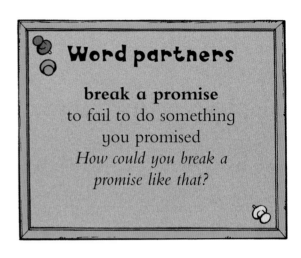

Word partners

break a promise
to fail to do something
you promised
*How could you break a
promise like that?*

swear
to make a promise that something
is true, sometimes officially
*If I tell you a secret, do you swear not
to tell anyone?*

undertake
an official or legal promise
*The government has undertaken to
reduce poverty.*

A B C D E F G H I J K L M

vow

to make a serious promise or
decision
We vowed to be friends forever.

• **to fulfil a promise**

deliver

to do what you promised
Will they be able to deliver as promised?

go through with

to keep a promise, especially if you
no longer want to or think you can
*I don't think we can win the match but
we will go through with it anyway.*

stand by/stick to

to keep a promise even though the
situation has changed
*The directors said they would stand by
their promise.*

In other words

promise the earth (idiom)
to promise something that is
impossible
*My brother promised us the earth if we
would just be quiet.*

Proud

arrogant
overly proud of yourself, acting as though you are more important than other people
He is arrogant and rude.

bigheaded
feeling that you are very clever, especially because you have been successful at something
Since Jemma was made head girl, she's acting really bigheaded.

▶ bigheaded

boastful
talking proudly about things you have or have done
He can't open his mouth without being boastful.

conceited
overly proud of your abilities, looks or the things you have done
It's difficult to be friends with a conceited person.

haughty
proud and unfriendly
I thought she was haughty but she's really just shy.

pompous
trying to impress people with how important you are
It was a pompous speech.

The opposite of proud is ashamed.

A B C D E F G H I J K L M

conceited • haughty • pompous
smug • snobbish • superior • vain

In other words

too big for your boots (idiom)
believing that you are more important than you really are
You're getting too big for your boots. You can't tell me what to do!

superior
thinking that you are better than other people
It's difficult to learn from people who think they are superior.

vain
thinking that you are very good-looking
Stop looking in the mirror, you vain thing!

smug
too pleased with yourself
He won't be so smug when he finds out that he came second this time.

snobbish
thinking that you are better than someone else because you are in a higher social position
Snobbish people aren't wanted here.

▶ vain

N O P Q R S T U V W X Y Z

apply
to put a liquid such as paint on something
Apply a thin layer and allow to dry completely.

deposit
to put something somewhere
He deposited the book on the table with a thump.

▲ deposit

lay
to put something down flat on a surface
Lay the coats on the bed, please.

place
to put something somewhere carefully
Place the stencil on the paper.

position
to carefully move something into a certain position
Position the prism at an angle.

• **to put something against something else**

lean
to put something against a wall or other vertical surface
Lean the ladder against the wall.

prop
to lean something against something else for support
I'll prop my bike against the wall.

stand

to lean something against a wall so that it is nearly vertical
Stand the picture in the corner for a minute.

• **to put things on top of one another**

heap

to throw or drop things on top of each other in an untidy way
He just heaps his clothes on the floor.

pile

to put things on top of each other
Pile the books on the table.

stack

to put things carefully on top of one another
The CDs are stacked in the cupboard.

Can you unscramble these four words that mean 'put'?

1. lapce   2. tacks
3. yal   4. leip

Answers: 1. place 2. stack
3. lay 4. pile

▼ heap

Quiet

hushed
quiet on purpose
The conversation in the waiting room was hushed.

inaudible
so quiet that you cannot hear it
He spoke in an almost inaudible whisper.

low
quiet and deep
There was a low hum coming from the machine.

muffled
quiet and unclear or blurred
Their speech is muffled by the helmets they are wearing.

> The opposites of quiet are noisy and loud.

muted
quieter than usual
We could hear muted voices in the corridor.

silent
with no sound
Please be absolutely silent while we are recording.

◀ muffled

A B C D E F G H I J K L M

soft
quiet and pleasant
There is soft music playing in the background.

still
calm and quiet
The night was still and the sky was full of stars.

In other words
as quiet as a mouse (idiom)
very quiet
I didn't hear you come in, you were as quiet as a mouse.

Word partners

peace and quiet
usually used when someone wants to escape a noisy or stressful situation
I'm going out to get some peace and quiet.

subdued
quieter than usual because you are sad or worried
You seem a bit subdued today – are you okay?

taciturn
saying very little
He plays the part of a stern, taciturn man.

• not false

authentic
real or true
This is an authentic antique map.

bona fide
real and honest
Make sure it's a bona fide website before you buy anything online.

genuine
not a fake
Genuine leather lasts a long time.

true
not a lie
It's true, the dog really did eat my homework!

 true

The opposites of real are false and imaginary.

• real feelings

heartfelt
strong and truly meant
Please accept our heartfelt thanks.

sincere
real and truly felt
I trust her and think she is being completely sincere.

• existing, not imaginary

actual
real
Her nickname is Posh but her actual name is Victoria.

concrete
based on facts
Do the police have any concrete evidence?

solid
based on real facts
There is solid evidence that smoking is bad for you.

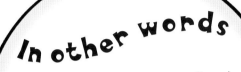

▲ concrete

In other words

The Real McCoy (idiom)
the real thing, not a copy
This comes from an American boxer, Kid McCoy, who was called The Real McCoy.

Remember

• **to remember**

recall
to remember
something
on purpose
*As I recall, we
said we'd meet at
the sports centre.*

recollect
to be able to remember something
*We went to Greece when I was a small
child but I don't recollect anything
about it.*

relive
to remember something
very clearly
*I relived missing that goal so
many times!*

◀ relive

reminisce
to think or talk about nice things
from the past
*My parents like to reminisce about
living in Africa.*

• **to cause someone to
remember**

prompt
to help someone remember
something, especially an actor
in a play
I'll prompt you if you forget the lines.

> The opposite of
> remember is forget.

A B C D E F G H I J K L M

remind

to make someone remember
something they need to
know or do
*Remind me to leave
a note for the
milkman.*

• **easy to
remember**

▶ haunting

haunting

easy to remember in a mysterious
way
*A beautiful, haunting melody
keeps going through my head.*

memorable

easy to remember because it is
very special
*Meeting the royal family was a
memorable moment.*

unforgettable

easy to remember because it
affected you a lot
*My first day at the new school
was unforgettable.*

In other words

something rings a bell (idiom)
something makes you partly
remember something
James? The name rings a bell.

rack your brains (idiom)
try to remember something
*Where are we going on
holiday? I've been racking
my brains trying to
remember.*

Rich

affluent
having a lot of money to buy things with
This is an affluent neighbourhood.

comfortable
having enough money
My grandparents have a comfortable life.

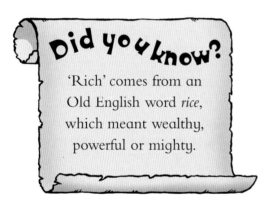

Did you know?

'Rich' comes from an Old English word *rice*, which meant wealthy, powerful or mighty.

flush
having more money than you usually have
I'll treat you − I'm flush right now.

prosperous
successful and having a lot of money
The town has become prosperous since the factory was built.

▶ flush

A B C D E F G H I J K L M

In other words

to be rolling in it (idiom)
to be very rich
Most pop stars are absolutely rolling in it!

wealthy
rich
They are a wealthy family and they're very generous.

well-heeled
having a lot of money and nice clothes
They look well-heeled.

well-off
having more money than most people
They're quite a well-off couple.

• people who are rich

a man/woman of means
a person who is rich and has property
The racehorse owner is a man of means.

the haves
people who have money
Unfortunately, there are still the haves and have-nots.

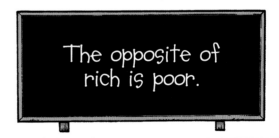

The opposite of rich is poor.

N O P Q R S T U V W X Y Z

Right

accepted • accurate • appropriate

accepted
approved or agreed that something
is right
*It is an accepted fact that the world is
not flat.*

The opposite of
right is wrong.

In other words

**to be in the right place at the
right time** (idiom)
to be in a place or a position where
something good is offered
*She's so lucky – always in the right
place at the right time.*

accurate
completely correct and true
*You have to type in web
addresses accurately.*

appropriate
right for a certain situation
*It's not appropriate to wear pyjamas
to school.*

apt
exactly right or suitable for
a situation
*Several pupils made apt remarks during
the discussion.*

A B C D E F G H I J K L M

correct
with no mistakes
Use the key to check that your answers are correct.

just
fair, morally right
It was a just punishment for the crime.

proper
right or correct
Put the books in the proper order.

suitable
right for a particular situation or time
Trainers aren't suitable shoes to wear to a wedding.

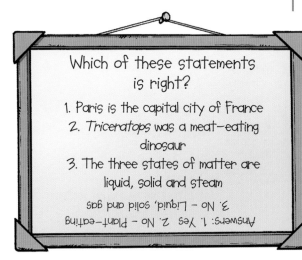

Which of these statements is right?

1. Paris is the capital city of France
2. *Triceratops* was a meat-eating dinosaur
3. The three states of matter are liquid, solid and steam

Answers: 1. Yes 2. No – Plant-eating 3. No – Liquid, solid and gas

▶ suitable

fitting
suitable or right for a particular situation
The poem was fitting for the ceremony.

Run

bolt
to run or move quickly because you are frightened
The horse bolted when the bell rang.

▼ bolt

dash
to run fast for a short distance
It was raining so we dashed to the car.

flee
to run away from danger
The children were fleeing from the monsters.

gallop
to run quickly with big steps
He galloped around the house.

jog
to run quite slowly for quite a long way
Mum jogs three times a week.

lope
to run with long, relaxed strides
The highjumper loped up to the bar and sprang over it with ease.

 flee

A B C D E F G H I J K L M

race

to run fast, especially against someone in a competition
We raced around the school field as fast as we could.

rush

move quickly to get somewhere or do something in a hurry
Mum was rushing around the house looking for her keys.

sprint

to run as fast as you can
The team of athletes sprinted around the track.

tear

to run fast without watching where you're going
He tore around the corner of the building and straight into the teacher.

▲ race

Word partners

run for cover
to move quickly to find shelter
As the rain began, we ran for cover.

Sad

dejected • depressed • desolate

down/low
sad and without energy
You might feel a little bit down after you've had flu.

fed-up
unhappy and annoyed or bored
I'm fed-up waiting for you.

▶ glum

glum
sad-looking
Why the glum face?

homesick
sad because you are away from home and miss the people there
You'll be homesick for the first few days.

unhappy
sad because of something that happens
What's wrong? You look unhappy.

• **very sad**

dejected
sad and disappointed
We were dejected when we lost.

The opposite of sad is happy.

A B C D E F G H I J K L M

depressed
feeling sad, usually for a long time
I was quite depressed when we first moved here but now I really like it.

desolate
extremely sad and lonely
The area has a flat, desolate landscape.

despondent
very sad and disappointed or not hopeful about the future
The team is despondent – they haven't won a match all year.

miserable
extremely sad
When you feel miserable you should just get up and do something.

In other words

sadder but wiser (idiom)
to have learned something from a bad or difficult experience
We came back from the match sadder but wiser.

consistent
steady, staying the same
Jess has made consistent improvement this term.

verbatim
in exactly the same words as the original
It is a verbatim account of the trial.

word for word
using exactly the same words
She repeated his speech, word for word.

• something that is the same as something else

carbon copy
exactly like another thing
The puppies are carbon copies of their mother.

▼ carbon copy

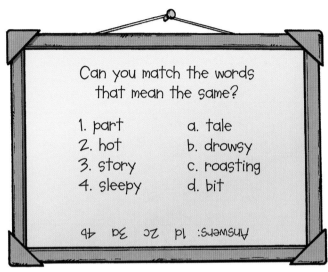

Can you match the words
that mean the same?

1. part   a. tale
2. hot   b. drowsy
3. story   c. roasting
4. sleepy   d. bit

Answers: 1d 2c 3a 4b

equivalent
something that has the same amount or size as something else
Do you know what the equivalent of £10 is in euros?

identical
exactly the same
That jacket is identical to mine.

synonym
a word that means the same as another word
Sidewalk is the American synonym of pavement.

counterpart
someone who has the same position as someone else
The minister met his UK counterpart.

duplicate
something that is an exact copy of something else
Please keep a duplicate of the letter.

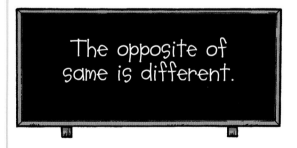

The opposite of
same is different.

N O P Q R S T U V W X Y Z

Say

blurt out • comment • exclaim • hint • mention

blurt out

to say something without thinking
He blurted out the answer.

hint

to say something indirectly
Mr Hunt hinted that there would be a test.

▶ blurt out

comment

to give an opinion
The captain commented on each player's performance.

exclaim

to say something loudly or suddenly
"This ride is fantastic!" she exclaimed.

mention

to say a little bit about a fact
The head mentioned that there would be new pupils this term.

A B C D E F G H I J K L M

In other words

it goes without saying
(idiom)
so obvious that something does not actually have to be said
It goes without saying that he'll do a good job.

mumble
to say something unclearly
Don't mumble when you're on stage, speak clearly.

▶ whisper

mutter
to say something quietly, especially if you are complaining
One of the players muttered something about the referee.

remark
to say what you think about something
The reporter remarked on how good our school's website is.

tell
to say something to someone
Please don't tell anyone.

whisper
to say something very softly
You play the game by whispering the sentence to the person next to you.

behind someone's back
done without telling someone
Friends don't do things behind your back.

cagey
not willing to tell other people your plans
Dad's being a bit cagey about where we're going on holiday – he wants it to be a surprise.

clandestine
something that is secret and sometimes illegal
The group holds clandestine meetings.

In other words

between you, me and the gatepost (idiom)
what you say when you tell someone something you don't want anyone else to know
Now, this is just between you, me and the gatepost.

clandestine • concealed • confidential • covert
furtive • hidden • hush-hush • in private

Word partners

keep a secret
to not tell anyone a secret
someone has told you
Can you keep a secret?

concealed
not showing
The microphone is concealed in a lamp.

confidential
private
The report is highly confidential.

covert
done in a secret way
We are involved in covert operations.

furtive
in a secret way
It was a quick, furtive pass.

hidden
not shown or visible
There's a message hidden in the book.

hush-hush
very secret
The plans are all very hush-hush.

in private
done where other people cannot
see or hear
They will discuss it in private.

The opposite of
secret is public.

N   O   P   Q   R   S   T   U   V   W   X   Y   Z

catnap
a very short sleep, usually not very deep
Why don't you have a quick catnap before we leave for the airport?

The opposite of asleep is awake.

doze
to sleep lightly
I was just dozing in front of the TV.

drop off
to go to sleep easily
I dropped off as soon as my head hit the pillow.

drift off
to go to sleep slowly
Be quiet, we're hoping the baby will drift off.

hibernate (for animals)
to go to sleep during the winter
Bears sometimes hibernate in caves.

kip
a short sleep
Why don't you have a kip in the car?

▶ drift off

nap
a short sleep, usually in the afternoon
Grandma has a nap after lunch.

slumber
sleep
The princess ate the apple and fell into a deep slumber.

Word partners

light sleeper
someone whose sleep is easily disturbed
Mum's a light sleeper.

In other words

to sleep like a log
(idiom)
to sleep very well
Did you get some sleep?
Yeah, I slept like a log!

snooze
a short, light sleep
Dad had a snooze while we went out for a walk.

dainty
small and delicate
The doll has dainty hands.

The opposite of small is large.

little
not big
They live in a sweet little cottage.

meagre
not enough, too little
The farmers try to survive on their meagre harvest.

miniature
much smaller than normal
There is a miniature town in Denmark.

minuscule
very small
A baby panda is minuscule compared to its mother.

minute
very small and difficult to see
A cat's whiskers are covered in minute sensors.

▶ puny

puny
small and weak
Pat Rafter was puny when he was a boy.

In other words

small world
something you say when you meet someone who knows a person or a place you know, and you are surprised
I don't believe you've met Sally too — what a small world!

• **become smaller**

shrink
to get smaller, often because of the effects of water or heat
My T-shirt shrank in the wash — it's too small now.

▶ shrink

tiny
very small
Coral reefs are made up of thousands of tiny animals.

shrivel
to get smaller and drier
Tomatoes shrivel up in very hot sun.

Smile

• to smile because you are happy

beam
to smile a big smile for a long time, usually because you are proud of something or someone
The parents beamed as their children went up to receive their prizes.

face lights up
to look happy suddenly
Their faces lit up as soon as they saw the lights on the tree.

The opposite of smile is frown.

Did you know?

In Old English, 'smirk' was the word for 'smile', but not in the unpleasant way that we understand it now.

grin
to suddenly break into a wide, happy smile
They grinned and waved when they saw us.

to break into a smile
to suddenly start smiling
She broke into a smile when she heard the good news.

• to smile in an unpleasant way

simper
to smile in a foolish, annoying way
The student simpered at the teacher.

smirk
to smile in a nasty way because you are pleased about someone else's bad luck
What are you smirking about?

sneer
to smile in an unpleasant way that shows that you don't respect someone or something
The giant sneered at the children as he passed by.

In other words

to grin like a Cheshire cat (idiom)
to smile very widely because you're pleased about something
This comes from a character in Lewis Carroll's book *Alice's Adventures in Wonderland*. Alice goes to a land where nothing is normal and she meets many strange characters. The Cheshire cat is one of these. He fades away as Alice is talking to him. The only thing left is his grin, floating in the air.

N O P Q R S T U V W X Y Z

Start

activate • begin • commence • embark on

activate
to start something happening or working
The machine is activated by pressing this button.

The opposites of start are finish and end.

In other words

to give someone a head start (idiom)
to give someone an advantage
The hare was so confident of winning the race, he gave the tortoise a head start.

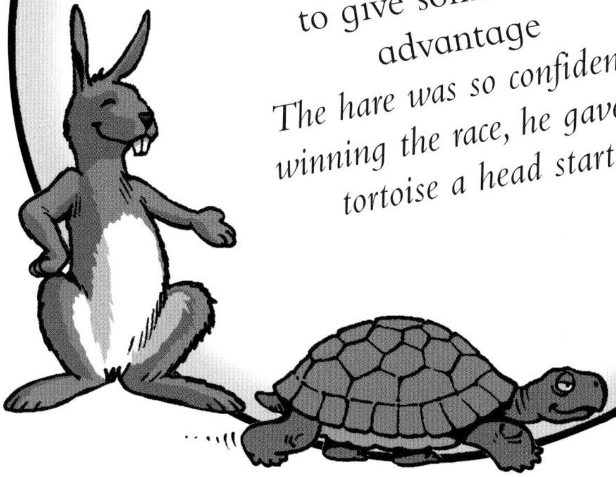

begin
to start doing something
You should begin the letter with 'Dear Sir'.

commence
to start or begin
The ceremony will now commence.

embark on
to start a big, important job or a journey
Our school is embarking on a big recycling project.

initiate
to start something such as a discussion about something
A neighbouring country initiated the peace talks.

▼ launch

launch
to start something publicly
The ship was launched by the mayoress.

open
to begin to be shown, such as a film
We want to see the film when it opens.

set in motion
to start something like a process that will take a long time
The plan has been set in motion.

• **to start something in an organization**

establish
to start something permanent
Oxford University was established more than 800 years ago.

found
to start something like a company or city
The company was founded in 1995.

set up
to make all the plans to start something
We've set up everything.

Steal

burglar • burgle • kleptomaniac • loot • mug

• to steal

burgle
to steal things from
a place such as a
house or office
*Our house was burgled
last night.*

▶ burgle

loot
to steal things from shops when the
police are busy because something
else is happening
Shops were looted in the riots.

mug
to attack and steal from someone
in the street
*The man was mugged as he walked
home from work.*

poach
to catch animals without
permission
Poaching is a problem in Africa.

rob
to steal something from
a person or place
An armed gang robbed the bank.

shoplift
to steal things from a shop
A boy was caught shoplifting.

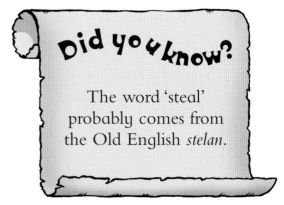

Did you know?
The word 'steal'
probably comes from
the Old English *stelan*.

In other words

tea leaf
cockney rhyming slang for 'thief'.

daylight robbery (idiom)
very expensive
These prices are daylight robbery.

• **people who steal**

burglar
a person who steals things from a building
The burglar got in through a window.

kleptomaniac
a person who is unable to stop stealing
Kleptomaniacs need professional help.

mugger
a person who steals money from people by attacking them in the street
The mugger was sent to jail for several months.

robber
a person who steals things from a public place
The robbers wore masks.

shoplifter
a person who steals when they are in shops
The CCTVs are there to stop shoplifters.

thief
a general word for a person who steals things
Car thieves can steal a car very quickly.

Stop

abandon
to stop doing something before it
is finished because it is difficult
The team abandoned the search.

> The opposites of
> stop are start
> and begin.

cease
to stop happening
Fighting has ceased.

drop
to stop doing something because
it does not seem like a good thing
to do
*We've decided to drop plans for a concert
until after the holidays.*

end
to finish or stop
How does the story end?

finish
to stop doing something because
it is complete
When you finish the test you may leave.

In other words

**to stop someone in
their tracks** (idiom)
to surprise someone suddenly
so they stop what
they are doing
*A loud noise stopped
us in our tracks.*

halt

halt
to stop moving
The procession halted.

pause
to stop temporarily
Pause, take a breath and then sing the next part.

quit
to stop doing something
Quit running, walk!

retire
to stop working
Grandma retired when she was 60.

stall
to stop, usually an engine in a car or plane, because there is not enough power
Our car sometimes stalls on hills.

N O P Q R S T U V W X Y Z

anecdote
a short, usually funny, story
He told an anecdote about his first day at school.

epic
a very long story about past times told in a poem, book or film
Beowulf *is an epic poem that was written more than 1000 years ago.*

fable
a story with a moral message, usually with animal characters
Aesop's Fables *were not written down at first.*

legend
a very old magical story
The legend of William Tell is about a man who had to shoot an apple off his son's head.

In other words

to cut a long story short
(idiom)
to tell the main facts of a story leaving out most of the details
Anyway, to cut a long story short, we decided to come home early.

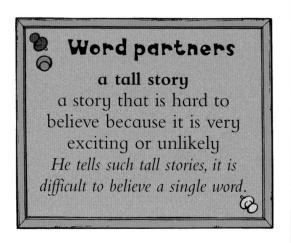

Word partners

a tall story
a story that is hard to believe because it is very exciting or unlikely
He tells such tall stories, it is difficult to believe a single word.

myth

an ancient story
There are famous myths from ancient Greece, Rome and Scandinavia.

novel

a book that is about imaginary people and things
Would you like to borrow it — it's an amazing novel?

saga

a story about a long period of time
A saga is often written about one family.

tale

an exciting story
My uncle tells tales about his adventures in Africa.

yarn

a long story about exciting things that are hard to believe
'Spinning yarns' means telling people stories that aren't true.

▶ novel

Stupid

absurd • daft • dim • foolish

• words for describing ideas or other things that are not sensible

absurd
completely stupid
The plan is absolutely absurd – it'll never work.

daft
childishly stupid but sometimes funny
Michael is very bright but sometimes he has daft ideas.

▶ daft

foolish
stupid in a way that could cause problems in the future
I think it would be foolish to plant the seeds this early.

idiotic
very stupid, sometimes risky
He's always taking idiotic chances – he's a real daredevil.

ridiculous
unbelievably stupid
Don't be ridiculous – we can't be in two places at the same time.

In other words

to play the fool (idiom)
to act in a silly way to make people laugh
Sam is always playing the fool.

unwise
stupid in a way that could cause problems
It is unwise to swim right after eating a big meal.

• **not intelligent**

dim
slow to understand or learn
Now I get it, sorry to be so dim!

thick
not intelligent at all
He's not thick, just a little confused.

silly
childishly stupid, sometimes in a funny way
We played a few silly games but they were fun.

The opposites of stupid are sensible and intelligent.

Surprised

- surprised

▶ amazed

astounded
very surprised
We were astounded by the news.

shocked
very surprised by something bad
We were shocked by their behaviour.

amazed
so surprised you can't quite
believe what's happened
*We were amazed by some
of his card tricks.*

astonished
very surprised that
something has happened
I'm astonished he won.

In other words
**you could have knocked me
down with a feather!** (idiom)
something you say when you are
really surprised
*You could have
knocked me down
with a feather when
the lights came on and
everybody shouted
"Surprise"!*

A B C D E F G H I J K L M

speechless
to be so surprised that you can't talk
When they told us the price we were speechless.

taken aback
so surprised that you don't know what to say
I was really taken aback by their comments.

• **surprising**

speechless

incredible
unbelievably surprising
He is an incredible runner.

marvellous
wonderful and surprising
The wildlife photography in this book is marvellous.

staggering
extremely surprising in a good or bad way
They spent a staggering amount of money.

stunning
very surprising
The special effects are stunning.

N O P Q R S T U V W X Y Z

carry

to take something from
one place to another
*The helicopter carried fresh
supplies of food and water
to the camp.*

convey

to take something such
as liquid, electricity or
gas from one place to
another
*The blood is conveyed from
the heart through the body's
arteries.*

deliver

to take letters, parcels,
newspapers and other
things to a place
*We had to deliver all of the
Christmas cards on foot.*

In other words

**you can take a horse to water
but you can't make him drink**
(saying)
this means you can give someone the
chance to do something but you can't
make them take it.

fetch

to go and get something and take it back to where you started
Could you fetch the children from school on your way back?

transport

to take lots of people or things from one place to another
Oil is transported in tankers.

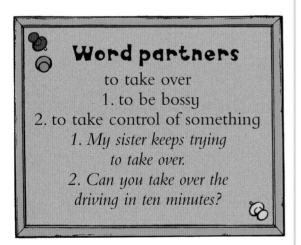

Word partners

to take over
1. to be bossy
2. to take control of something
1. *My sister keeps trying to take over.*
2. *Can you take over the driving in ten minutes?*

The opposite of take is give.

• **to take someone somewhere**

guide

to take someone to a place you know well
We were guided around the exhibition.

lead

to take someone somewhere by going in front of them
They led us out of the cave.

shepherd

to take a group of people somewhere
I was shepherded inside the house.

Talk

blab • chat • converse • gossip

blab

to talk about something that you are not supposed to mention

Who blabbed?

chat

to talk in a friendly way

We were just chatting about what we did in the summer holidays.

converse

to talk to someone

Parents' day is a time when teachers and parents meet and converse.

◀ gossip

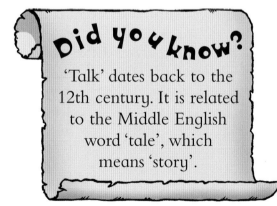

Did you know?

'Talk' dates back to the 12th century. It is related to the Middle English word 'tale', which means 'story'.

gossip

to talk about other people's lives

I could tell they were gossiping about something when we walked in.

natter

to talk about things for fun

We sat and nattered about our favourite bands all day long.

A B C D E F G H I J K L M

rabbit

to keep talking about something, usually boring

What are you rabbiting about now?

waffle

to talk about something without saying anything useful

He waffled on about badges.

Word partners

small talk

to make polite conversation about nothing in particular

The taxi driver made small talk as he drove us to the station.

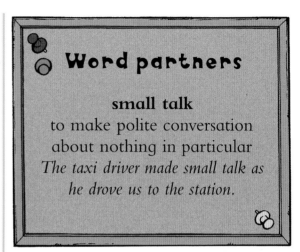

In other words

can talk the hind legs off a donkey
(idiom)
able to talk a lot
My Aunt Jo can talk the hind legs off a donkey.

witter

to talk for a long time without saying much

Jamie wittered on for hours.

Think

brood • consider • contemplate • meditate

brood
to keep thinking about something that upsets you
Don't just sit there brooding – do something about it.

◀ brood

consider
to think about something that you might do
We're considering going to France.

contemplate
to think seriously or deeply about something
They contemplated major changes.

meditate
to think deeply about something for a long time
Meditating each day is really relaxing.

ponder
to think about a difficult question or a problem
He looked at the iron gate and pondered his escape.

reckon
to think that something is right or true
I reckon they'll get here in time.

reflect
to think carefully about something
We need time to reflect on what has happened.

▶ meditate

A B C D E F G H I J K L M

regard
to have an opinion of someone or something
They don't think of it as work – they regard it as good fun.

wonder
to try to guess what is happening or what will happen
I wonder where they've got to?

Did you know?
'Use your loaf' is cockney rhyming slang. It comes from 'loaf of bread', which rhymes with 'head'.

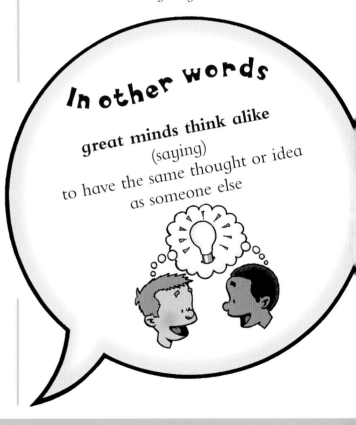

In other words

great minds think alike
(saying)
to have the same thought or idea as someone else

suspect
to think that something is probably true
I suspect there will be a question about gravity in the test.

Throw

bowl • chuck • fling • heave

bowl
to throw a ball at a batman
in cricket
Who's bowling for their team?

chuck
to throw something carelessly
Just chuck that stuff on the floor.

◀ chuck

fling
to throw or move
something forcefully
*She flung her scarf
around her neck.*

In other words

to throw in the towel (idiom)
to stop doing something because
you don't think you can succeed
*The boxer grew tired of fighting
and threw in the towel.*

heave
to throw something heavy
*They heaved the sacks onto the
back of the truck.*

hurl
to throw something forcefully
and violently
He hurled the spear at the target.

lob
to throw something high into the air
We lobbed the ball over the fence.

pass
to throw the ball to another player on the same team
Quick, pass it over here!

▲ pass

pelt
to throw things at someone or something
The clowns pelted each other with tomatoes.

sling
to throw something carelessly
Don't just sling the book on the table.

toss
to throw something with a quick, small movement
Toss me that cushion, will you?

◀ pelt

N O P Q R S T U V W X Y Z

Tired

beat • drained • drowsy • exhausted

beat
so tired that you want to stop
what you're doing
Sorry, I've got to rest, I'm beat.

drained
tired, without any energy left
*I felt drained after
karate class.*

drowsy
tired and sleepy
*The heat made us drowsy
so we went up to bed.*

 drained

In other words

**to be sick and tired of
something** (idiom)
to feel angry or bored because
something has been happening
for a long time
I'm sick and tired of all this ironing.

A B C D E F G H I J K L M

exhausted
very tired after doing something that used up your energy
You walked all the way? You must be exhausted.

flagging
starting to lose energy
During the tie-break, you could see she was flagging.

▲ flagging

shattered
very tired
I'm absolutely shattered. Is it okay if we stay at home tonight?

sleepy
ready to go to sleep
Go on up to bed, you look sleepy.

▶ sleepy

tired/worn out
very tired after a lot of physical effort
That's it. We've got to stop running — I'm tired out.

weary
to feel tired after doing something for a long period of time
We'd been walking all day and were very weary.

N O P Q R S T U V W X Y Z

Travel

• to travel

▶ commute

commute
to travel to and from work
Dad commutes to the city every day.

explore
to travel to find out more about
a place
*We'll have time to really explore
the island.*

wander
to travel round without a plan
*Dad hired a car and we just wandered
along the coast for a week.*

• types of travel

crossing
a trip in a boat or a ship across
water from one side to the other
*It was a rough crossing because
of the storm.*

excursion
a short trip to visit a place
We have an excursion every term.

journey
travel from one place to another,
usually far away
The journey was long but interesting.

outing
a short trip or visit to a place,
usually nearby
*There is a class outing on Friday to
the castle.*

A B C D E F G H I J K L M

journey • outing • tour • trip • voyage • wander

1. Who travelled to the South Pole in 1911?
2. Which space mission travelled to the Moon in 1969?
3. Which aircraft travelled faster than the speed of sound?

Answers: 1. Roald Amundsen 2. Apollo 11 3. Concorde

voyage
a long journey in a ship or spacecraft
We set out on our voyage across the ocean.

tour
a visit to and around a place
We went on a tour of the city.

trip
travel to a place, usually for a short time
Mum is on a business trip.

▶ voyage

absorb
to learn and understand new information
There was a lot of information to absorb on the first day.

appreciate
to understand someone's feelings or their situation
Teachers appreciate that a child's first day at school can be confusing.

Did you know?
We can understand Egyptian hieroglyphs because of the Rosetta Stone, found in 1799. It is an ancient stone with the same message carved in three different writing systems.

comprehend
to understand something difficult or complicated
They were too young to comprehend what was happening.

▶ digest

digest
to think carefully about and understand new information
They'll need time to digest the report.

follow
to understand something that has more than one point
Do you follow so far?

get
to understand a story, joke or the reason for something
Sorry, but I didn't get that joke.

> The opposite of understand is misunderstand.

grasp
to clearly understand something difficult
They didn't grasp the full importance of the new law.

make sense of
to understand something because you have thought about it
I'm just beginning to make sense of how this computer game works.

realise
to understand something that you didn't before
I didn't realise we were supposed to complete all four questions.

see
to understand what something means or the reason for it
So you see, we need to keep a clear record of each student's project.

Can you understand this text message?

C U L8R R U OK?

Answer: See you later. Are you ok?

- value

advantage
something that is valuable and
will help you succeed
We have a great advantage.

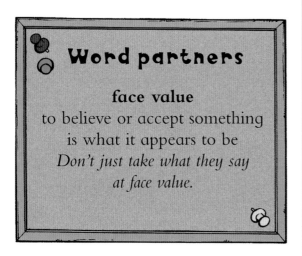

Word partners

face value
to believe or accept something
is what it appears to be
*Don't just take what they say
at face value.*

benefit
something that helps you
We have the benefit of good facilities.

esteem
respect and admiration
Dad's boss holds him in high esteem.

▶ esteem

merit
valuable qualities of something
or someone
The idea has great merit.

worth
the value of something
The thieves took £1000 worth of CDs.

• to value

cherish
to value or love something a lot
Mum cherishes the photos of when we were little.

prize
to feel that something is important or valuable
Grandad prizes his roses.

rate
to give a value to something
I rated the jewellery extremely highly.

treasure
to feel that something is very valuable and gives you a lot of pleasure
We treasure our memories.

• valuable

precious
extremely valuable, usually because it is something that is expensive or rare
Diamonds, emeralds and rubies are all kinds of precious stones.

priceless
so valuable that no price can be put on it
There are lots of priceless Roman artefacts in the museum.

◀ cherish

Very

absolutely/completely
in every way
I completely forgot to send her a birthday card last year.

decidedly
very much, in an obvious way
The entire team are playing decidedly better this season.

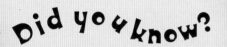

Did you know?

We don't use 'very' with words that already have a strong meaning. For example, we don't say "I was very astounded." Instead we say something such as, "I was completely astounded."

The opposites of very are hardly and slightly.

highly
very
The computer programmers are highly skilled people.

noticeably
very, in a way that is easy for people to see
The sports centre is noticeably busier in the school holidays.

particularly
especially
The judges were particularly impressed with her gymnastic routine.

A B C D E F G H I J K L M

quite
very much
They are twins but their personalities are quite different.

▼ really

really
very
It's really hot in here – can I open the window?

remarkably
very much so, in a surprising way
The results were remarkably good this year.

terribly
very, usually used only in spoken English
I'm terribly sorry I was late – I overslept.

truly
very
I'm truly sorry about the broken window.

▶ truly

Wait

await • delay • hesitate

await
to wait for something
The court is awaiting the jury's decision.

hold on
used to tell someone to wait for
a short time
*Hold on a minute, I'll just check
for you.*

queue
to stand in a line
waiting for
something
*We had to queue
for two hours.*

* to wait or make someone wait
before doing something

delay
to cause something to be late
We were delayed by traffic.

▶ delay

In other words

he who hesitates is lost
(saying)
If you don't do something when you get the chance, you might not get the chance again.

linger
to wait for extra time before leaving a place
Fans lingered, hoping to get an autograph.

pause
to wait for a while before continuing to do something
The lion paused and looked around.

hesitate
to wait a little while before doing something, usually because you are not sure
Lily hesitated before choosing which library book she wanted.

e	q	r	t	i	r
t	u	o	q	o	e
a	o	d	u	s	g
t	o	e	e	s	n
i	s	l	u	e	i
s	c	a	e	t	l
e	t	y	i	y	u
h	o	p	q	u	e

Find four words that mean 'wait'. They could be backwards!

Answers: hesitate delay linger queue

Walk

creep • hike • limp • march

creep
to walk quietly, slowly and secretly
*We crept up and jumped in front
of them.*

hike
to walk a long way, usually in
the country
*We hiked up the hill and found a
good place for our picnic.*

limp
to walk dragging one foot because
it hurts
*David limped slowly off the football
pitch.*

march
to walk together using strong,
regular steps
*The group of soldiers marched proudly
past the flag.*

▲ creep

stride
to walk confidently with big steps
He strode into the room.

stroll
to walk slowly and comfortably
We strolled through the park.

tiptoe

to walk on your toes, trying not to make a noise
I tiptoed past their room.

▲ tiptoe

trek

to walk a long way, especially in hills or mountains
I'd like to trek in the Himalayas.

wade

to walk through water
I waded into the pond to get the ball.

wander

to walk without a purpose or because you are lost
They wandered in the forest for hours before they found the camp.

In other words

walk the plank (idiom)
to be forced to do something
This comes from the great age of sailing ships, when someone who did something wrong would have to walk out on a long board (plank) and jump into the water.

Want

aspire to • crave • desire • fancy

aspire to

to want or hope to do something or be something, and work towards it
The story is about a girl who aspired to stardom.

▶ crave

crave

to want something so much that you can't think about anything else
I woke up craving chocolate.

desire

to want something very much
You can have whatever you desire. There's something for everyone.

fancy

to want something
I fancy a walk, want to come?

hanker after

to think about something that you want but can't have
After a week at school, we were hankering after Mum's cooking.

◀ hanker after

long for

to want something very much
We long for the summer holidays.

A B C D E F G H I J K L M

wish for
to want something to happen
I wish they'd hurry up and get here.

▼ yearn for

a feeling of wanting something

impulse
a sudden feeling that you want
to do or have something without
thinking if it is a good idea
I bought this bag on impulse.

whim
a sudden feeling that you want
to do or have something
You can't get a puppy on a whim.

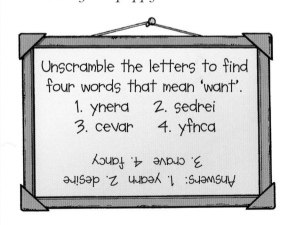

Unscramble the letters to find
four words that mean 'want'.
1. ynera   2. sedrei
3. cevar   4. yfnca

Answers: 1. yearn 2. desire
3. crave 4. fancy

yearn for
to want something so much that
you feel sad without it
The prisoner yearned for freedom.

Wet

clammy • damp • drenched • humid • moist

clammy
wet and sticky
When I'm nervous, the palms of my hands get clammy.

damp
slightly wet
These clothes are still damp from the rain.

drenched
extremely wet
The rain was so heavy we got absolutely drenched in no time.

moist
slightly wet
Keep the soil moist.

saturated
completely wet
The cloth is saturated, wring it out.

◀ clammy

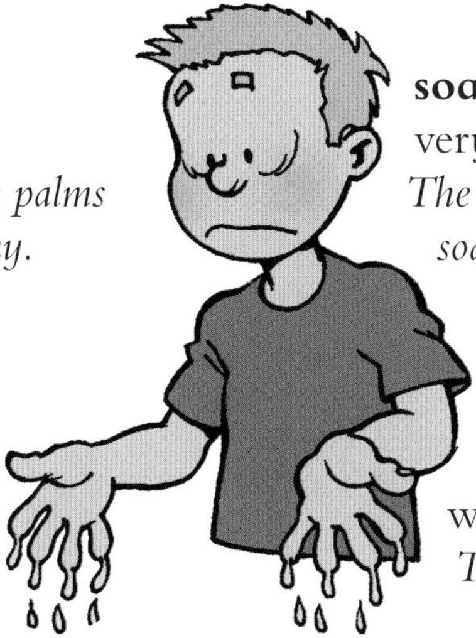

soaked
very wet
The cushions in the garden got soaked overnight.

sodden
wet and heavy
The bottom of the box is sodden.

Word partners

a wet blanket
someone who stops other people from having fun
Look, I don't mean to be a wet blanket but turn the music down.

The opposite of
wet is dry.

waterlogged
so wet that something cannot hold
more water
*The pitch is waterlogged, so the match
is postponed.*

• **wet weather**

humid
wet and hot
It is hot and humid this time of year.

muggy
unpleasantly wet and warm
We don't like playing when it's muggy.

In other words

wet behind the ears (idiom)
young and inexperienced
*It's his first day working here.
He's a little wet behind the ears.*

▫ a win

achievement
something that you
succeed in doing
*Setting a new school record
was an outstanding
achievement.*

conquest
a victory, usually if a
country takes control
of a place after winning
a battle
*The Norman Conquest was
led by William the Conqueror.*

In other words

**to win something
hands down** (idiom)
to win easily
Imogen won the race hands down!

The opposite of
win is lose.

landslide
when one side or candidate gets
many more votes than another
*The voting revealed that we had won
by a landslide.*

success
a win, especially in a series
of games, matches or fights
The match was our third success.

victory
a win, especially in a competition
or battle
*The streets were full of people celebrating
the victory.*

walkover
a very easy win, especially in sport
The set was a walkover for her.

• **to win**

sweep the board
to win all the points, medals or
prizes
*Our class swept the board at the sports
day competition.*

triumph
to win something
difficult or important
*It was a great triumph
for their team.*

win easily
to win a race or
game without
a lot of difficulty
*They won the first
few events quickly
and easily.*

◀ walkover

Work

labour
to work hard, usually doing something physical
The labour was long and hard.

push yourself
to force yourself to work hard
I had to push myself to finish.

▲ push yourself

slave away
to work extremely hard at something that you do not enjoy
The sailors slaved away at the oars.

to be industrious
to work very hard and get lots of things done
You've been very industrious.

toil
to do boring work for a long time
In colonial times, thousands of people toiled in the plantations.

◦ **a task**

drudgery
work that is physically hard and boring
Working in factories can sometimes be drudgery.

duties
things that you have to do as part of your job
Everyone in the class has different duties.

grind
boring work
Memorising your times tables is a grind but it pays off.

▶ grind

job
the work that a person does to get money
Mum is looking for a new job.

In other words

beaver away at (idiom)
to work very hard at something
He beavered away at his homework for hours.

This comes from the way beavers work when they build complicated dams.

Young

• **a young person**

adolescent
a young person who is developing into an adult
Teenagers are adolescents.

infant
a baby or young child
I don't remember living there because I was an infant when we left.

◀ infant

juvenile
a young person
There are special rules for juveniles.

kid
a child
Don't be too hard on him – he's just a kid.

Unscramble the letters to find four names of young animals.

1. legipt   2. loaf
3. eldpoat   4. lcfa

Answers: 1. piglet 2. foal
3. tadpole 4. calf

minor
a legal term for a person who is not an adult
I'm afraid that minors must be accompanied by an adult.

A B C D E F G H I J K L M

• **young**

little
a sister or brother who is younger than you
My little brother is learning to walk.

◄ small

The opposite of young is old.

Word partners

young at heart
to feel very young, even if you are not
I may be getting older, but I'm young at heart.

small
young, usually less than ten years of age
Dad says that when he was small, he couldn't swim.

Index

All the synonyms and their headwords in your book are listed alphabetically here. Simply look up the word you want to use – the headword for that entry is listed opposite in **bold** type.

Aa

a breeze	see **Easy**
a doddle	see **Easy**
a man/woman of means	see **Rich**
abandon	see **Stop**
abhor	see **Hate**
absolutely	see **Very**
absorb	see **Understand**
absurd	see **Stupid**
accelerate	see **Fast**
accepted	see **Right**
accurate	see **Right**
achievement	see **Win**
activate	see **Start**
actual	see **Real**
adolescent	see **Young**
adore	see **Love**
advantage	see **Value**
affectionate	see **Love**
affluent	see **Rich**
afraid	see **Frightened**
ageing	see **Old**

ajar	see **Open**
alias	see **Name**
allowance	see **Money**
amazed	see **Surprised**
amazing	see **Good**
amiable	see **Friend**
amusing	see **Funny**
ancient	see **Old**
anecdote	see **Story**
animosity	see **Hate**
annoyed	see **Angry**
antique	see **Old**
appalling	see **Bad**
apply	see **Put**
appreciate	see **Know**
appreciate	see **Understand**
appropriate	see **Right**
apt	see **Right**
arrogant	see **Proud**
artificial	see **Pretend**
aspire to	see **Want**
assemble	see **Make**
assignment	see **Job**
assure	see **Promise**
astonished	see **Surprised**
astounded	see **Surprised**
authentic	see **Real**
average	see **Ordinary**
await	see **Wait**
award	see **Give**
awkward	see **Difficult**

Bb

backbreaking	see **Difficult**
baking	see **Hot**
balmy	see **Hot**
banal	see **Ordinary**
be aware of	see **Know**
be close to	see **Love**
be devoted to	see **Love**
be familiar with	see **Know**
be fond of	see **Love**
be well-up on	see **Know**
beam	see **Smile**
beat	see **Tired**
begin	see **Start**
behind someone's back	see **Secret**
benefit	see **Value**
bequeath	see **Give**
bicker	see **Argue**
big headed	see **Proud**
bit	see **Part**
blab	see **Talk**
bland	see **Ordinary**
blaring	see **Loud**
bluff	see **Pretend**
blunder	see **Mistake**
blurt out	see **Say**
boastful	see **Proud**
boiling	see **Hot**
bolt	see **Eat**
bolt	see **Run**

bona fide	see **Real**
bonus	see **Payment**
booming	see **Loud**
bound	see **Jump**
bowl	see **Throw**
brainy	see **Clever**
branch	see **Part**
brand name	see **Name**
break into a smile	see **Smile**
brand new	see **New**
bribe	see **Payment**
bright	see **Clever**
brilliant	see **Good**
bring	see **Carry**
brisk	see **Fast**
broke	see **Poor**
brood	see **Think**
buddy	see **Friend**
budge	see **Move**
build	see **Make**
burglar	see **Steal**
burgle	see **Steal**
burst out laughing	see **Laugh**

Cc

cackle	see **Laugh**
cagey	see **Secret**
can't bear/stand	see **Frightened**
carbon copy	see **Same**
care about	see **Love**
carry	see **Take**

cash	see **Money**	commonplace	see **Ordinary**
catch	see **Problem**	commute	see **Travel**
catnap	see **Sleep**	companion	see **Friend**
cease	see **Stop**	completely	see **Very**
central	see **Important**	complication	see **Problem**
challenging	see **Difficult**	component	see **Part**
change	see **Money**	comprehend	see **Understand**
character	see **Person**	concealed	see **Secret**
chat	see **Talk**	conceited	see **Proud**
cheerful	see **Happy**	conceive of	see **Imagine**
cherish	see **Love**	concoct	see **Make**
chew	see **Eat**	concrete	see **Real**
chilling	see **Frightened**	confidential	see **Secret**
chilly	see **Cold**	conquest	see **Win**
chore	see **Job**	consider	see **Think**
chortle	see **Laugh**	consistent	see **Same**
chuck	see **Throw**	consult	see **Ask**
chuckle	see **Laugh**	consume	see **Eat**
circle	see **Friend**	contemplate	see **Think**
clammy	see **Wet**	contempt	see **Hate**
clandestine	see **Secret**	content	see **Happy**
clash	see **Argue**	contrast with	see **Different**
close	see **Near**	converse	see **Talk**
clown	see **Funny**	convey	see **Take**
code name	see **Name**	cool	see **Cold**
coins	see **Money**	correct	see **Right**
comedian	see **Funny**	counterpart	see **Same**
comfortable	see **Rich**	covert	see **Secret**
comical	see **Funny**	crave	see **Want**
commence	see **Start**	create	see **Make**
comment	see **Say**	creep	see **Walk**

critical	see **Important**
cross	see **Angry**
crossing	see **Travel**
cross-section	see **Part**
crowd	see **Friend**
crucial	see **Important**
crumb	see **Part**
cry	see **Call**
cunning	see **Clever**
currency	see **Money**

Dd

daft	see **Stupid**
dainty	see **Small**
damp	see **Wet**
dash	see **Fast**
dash	see **Run**
daydream	see **Imagine**
deafening	see **Loud**
debate	see **Argue**
decent	see **Good**
decidedly	see **Very**
dejected	see **Sad**
delay	see **Wait**
delighted	see **Happy**
deliver	see **Promise**
deliver	see **Take**
demanding	see **Difficult**
demolish	see **Eat**
deposit	see **Payment**
deposit	see **Put**

depressed	see **Sad**
deprived	see **Poor**
desire	see **Want**
desolate	see **Sad**
despise	see **Hate**
despondent	see **Sad**
destitute	see **Poor**
detest	see **Hate**
devour	see **Eat**
difficulty	see **Problem**
digest	see **Understand**
dilemma	see **Problem**
dim	see **Stupid**
disadvantaged	see **Poor**
dispute	see **Argue**
dissimilar	see **Different**
distinctive	see **Different**
distribute	see **Give**
diverse	see **Different**
donate	see **Give**
doting	see **Love**
down	see **Sad**
doze	see **Sleep**
drain	see **Drink**
drained	see **Tired**
draughty	see **Cold**
dreadful	see **Bad**
dreading	see **Frightened**
dream of	see **Imagine**
drenched	see **Wet**
drift off	see **Sleep**

drop	see **Stop**
drop off	see **Sleep**
drowsy	see **Sleep**
drudgery	see **Work**
duplicate	see **Same**
duties	see **Work**
duty	see **Job**

Ee

ear-splitting	see **Loud**
ecstatic	see **Happy**
effortless	see **Easy**
elderly	see **Old**
element	see **Part**
embark on	see **Start**
end	see **Stop**
enquire	see **Ask**
epic	see **Story**
equivalent	see **Same**
errand	see **Job**
error	see **Mistake**
essential	see **Important**
establish	see **Start**
esteem	see **Value**
everyday	see **Ordinary**
examine	see **Look**
excellent	see **Good**
exclaim	see **Say**
excursion	see **Travel**

exhausted	see **Tired**
expert	see **Know**
explore	see **Travel**

Ff

fable	see **Story**
face lights up	see **Smile**
fake	see **Pretend**
false	see **Pretend**
family	see **Person**
fancy	see **Want**
fantasise	see **Imagine**
fantastic	see **Good**
fashion	see **Make**
fault	see **Mistake**
fed up	see **Sad**
fee	see **Payment**
feed	see **Eat**
feel	see **Know**
fetch	see **Carry**
fetch	see **Take**
feud	see **Argue**
fiddly	see **Difficult**
fight	see **Argue**
figure	see **Money**
fine	see **Payment**
finish	see **Stop**
fitting	see **Right**
flagging	see **Tired**
flee	see **Run**
fling	see **Throw**

flush	see **Rich**
folk	see **Person**
follow	see **Understand**
foolish	see **Stupid**
force	see **Open**
form	see **Make**
fortune	see **Money**
found	see **Start**
fraction	see **Part**
freezing	see **Cold**
fresh	see **New**
frosty	see **Cold**
fun	see **Good**
furious	see **Angry**
furtive	see **Secret**

Gg

gaffe	see **Mistake**
gag	see **Joke**
gallop	see **Run**
gang	see **Friend**
gaze	see **Look**
generate	see **Make**
genuine	see **Real**
geriatric	see **Old**
get	see **Understand**
ghastly	see **Bad**
giggle	see **Laugh**
give your word	see **Promise**
glad	see **Happy**

glance	see **Look**
glare	see **Look**
glimpse	see **Look**
glum	see **Sad**
go through with	see **Promise**
gobble	see **Eat**
goof	see **Mistake**
goosepimples	see **Cold**
gossip	see **Talk**
grasp	see **Understand**
great	see **Good**
grin	see **Smile**
grind	see **Work**
gruelling	see **Difficult**
guarantee	see **Promise**
guffaw	see **Laugh**
guide	see **Take**
gulp	see **Drink**
guzzle	see **Drink**

Hh

hair-raising	see **Frightened**
hallucinate	see **Imagine**
halt	see **Stop**
hand	see **Give**
handy	see **Near**
hanker after	see **Want**
hard	see **Difficult**
hassle	see **Problem**
haughty	see **Proud**
haul	see **Carry**

haunting	see **Remember**
heap	see **Put**
heartfelt	see **Real**
heave	see **Throw**
hero/heroine	see **Person**
hesitate	see **Wait**
hibernate	see **Sleep**
hiccup	see **Problem**
hidden	see **Secret**
high-speed	see **Fast**
highly	see **Very**
hike	see **Walk**
hilarious	see **Funny**
hindrance	see **Problem**
hint	see **Say**
historic	see **Important**
hold on	see **Wait**
homesick	see **Sad**
hop	see **Jump**
hopeless	see **Bad**
hospitable	see **Friend**
human/human being	see **Person**
humanity	see **Person**
humankind	see **Person**
humid	see **Wet**
humorous	see **Funny**
hurdle	see **Jump**
hurdle	see **Problem**
hurl	see **Throw**
hushed	see **Quiet**
hush-hush	see **Secret**

Ii

identical	see **Same**
identity	see **Name**
idiotic	see **Stupid**
idiot-proof	see **Easy**
impersonate	see **Pretend**
impossible	see **Difficult**
imposter	see **Pretend**
impoverished	see **Poor**
impressive	see **Good**
impulse	see **Want**
in jest	see **Joke**
in private	see **Secret**
in the vicinity	see **Near**
inaudible	see **Quiet**
income	see **Money**
incredible	see **Good**
incredible	see **Surprised**
indignant	see **Angry**
individual	see **Different**
individual	see **Person**
inept	see **Bad**
infant	see **Young**
inferior	see **Bad**
ingredient	see **Part**
initial	see **Name**
initiate	see **Start**
innovative	see **New**
insincere	see **Pretend**
inspect	see **Look**
instalment	see **Payment**

intellectual	see **Clever**
intelligent	see **Clever**
interrogate	see **Ask**
interview	see **Ask**
irate	see **Angry**
irritated	see **Angry**

Jj
job	see **Work**
jog	see **Run**
joking	see **Joke**
jolly	see **Happy**
journey	see **Travel**
joyful	see **Happy**
just	see **Right**
just out	see **New**
juvenile	see **Young**

Kk
key	see **Important**
kid	see **Young**
kidding	see **Joke**
kin	see **Person**
kip	see **Sleep**
kleptomaniac	see **Steal**
knowledgeable	see **Clever**

Ll
| labour | see **Work** |
| landslide | see **Win** |

lap up	see **Drink**
latest	see **New**
launch	see **Start**
lay	see **Put**
lead	see **Take**
lean	see **Put**
leap	see **Jump**
legend	see **Story**
lift	see **Carry**
light-hearted	see **Funny**
limp	see **Walk**
linger	see **Wait**
little	see **Small**
little	see **Young**
livid	see **Angry**
loathe	see **Hate**
lob	see **Throw**
local	see **Near**
long for	see **Want**
loot	see **Steal**
lope	see **Run**
lovely	see **Good**
low	see **Quiet**
low	see **Sad**
lug	see **Carry**
lukewarm	see **Hot**

Mm
mad	see **Angry**
maiden name	see **Name**
major	see **Important**

make sense of	see **Understand**	mumble	see **Say**
make-believe	see **Pretend**	munch	see **Eat**
manufacture	see **Make**	mundane	see **Ordinary**
march	see **Walk**	muted	see **Quiet**
marvellous	see **Good**	mutter	see **Say**
marvellous	see **Surprised**	myth	see **Story**
masquerade	see **Pretend**		
mate	see **Friend**		
meagre	see **Small**		

Nn

meditate	see **Think**	name	see **Call**
memorable	see **Remember**	namesake	see **Name**
mention	see **Say**	nap	see **Sleep**
merit	see **Value**	natter	see **Talk**
miniature	see **Small**	naughty	see **Bad**
minor	see **Young**	nearby	see **Near**
minuscule	see **Small**	needy	see **Poor**
minute	see **Small**	neighbouring	see **Near**
miserable	see **Sad**	neighbourly	see **Friend**
mischievious	see **Bad**	neutral	see **Ordinary**
misjudge	see **Mistake**	newcomer	see **New**
mission	see **Job**	next	see **Near**
mix-up	see **Mistake**	nibble	see **Eat**
modern	see **New**	nice	see **Good**
moist	see **Wet**	nickname	see **Name**
money	see **Money**	noisy	see **Loud**
mould	see **Make**	normal	see **Ordinary**
muffled	see **Quiet**	not at all like	see **Different**
mug	see **Steal**	notable	see **Important**
mugger	see **Steal**	noticeably	see **Very**
muggy	see **Hot**	novel	see **New**
muggy	see **Wet**	novel	see **Story**

Oo

occupation	see **Job**
open	see **Start**
original	see **New**
outing	see **Travel**
outstanding	see **Good**
overjoyed	see **Happy**
oversight	see **Mistake**

Pp

painless	see **Easy**
pal	see **Friend**
panic-stricken	see **Frightened**
particularly	see **Very**
pass	see **Throw**
pass on	see **Give**
passionate	see **Love**
pause	see **Stop**
pause	see **Wait**
peek	see **Look**
peep	see **Look**
peer	see **Look**
pelt	see **Throw**
pen name	see **Name**
penetrating	see **Loud**
penniless	see **Poor**
petrified	see **Loud**
phone	see **Call**
pick a lock	see **Open**
picture	see **Imagine**

piercing	see **Loud**
pile	see **Put**
pioneering	see **New**
place	see **Put**
plead	see **Ask**
pleased	see **Happy**
pledge	see **Promise**
poach	see **Steal**
pocket money	see **Money**
polish off	see **Drink**
poll	see **Ask**
pompous	see **Proud**
ponder	see **Think**
portion	see **Part**
pose	see **Pretend**
position	see **Put**
pounce	see **Jump**
practical joke	see **Joke**
prank	see **Joke**
precious	see **Value**
present	see **Give**
priceless	see **Value**
prise	see **Open**
prize	see **Value**
produce	see **Make**
profession	see **Job**
project	see **Job**
prompt	see **Remember**
prop	see **Put**
proper	see **Right**
prosperous	see **Rich**

pseudonym	see **Name**
pump	see **Ask**
pun	see **Joke**
punch line	see **Joke**
puny	see **Small**
push yourself	see **Work**

Qq

quarrel	see **Argue**
quench	see **Drink**
query	see **Ask**
question	see **Ask**
queue	see **Wait**
quick	see **Clever**
quick	see **Fast**
quickly	see **Fast**
quit	see **Stop**
quite	see **Very**
quiz	see **Ask**

Rr

rabbit	see **Talk**
race	see **Run**
rapid	see **Fast**
rate	see **Value**
realise	see **Know**
realise	see **Understand**
really	see **Very**
recall	see **Remember**
recent	see **New**

reckon	see **Think**
recollect	see **Remember**
reflect	see **Think**
refund	see **Payment**
regard	see **Think**
relive	see **Remember**
relocate	scc **Move**
remark	see **Say**
remarkably	see **Very**
remind	see **Remember**
reminisce	see **Remember**
resentful	see **Angry**
retire	see **Stop**
reward	see **Give**
riddle	see **Joke**
ridiculous	see **Stupid**
ring	see **Call**
roar with laughter	see **Laugh**
roasting	see **Hot**
rob	see **Steal**
robber	see **Steal**
routine	see **Ordinary**
row	see **Argue**
rowdy	see **Loud**
rush	see **Fast**
rush	see **Run**

Ss

saga	see **Story**
salary	see **Payment**
saturated	see **Wet**

scalding	see **Hot**	sincere	see **Real**
scared	see **Frightened**	sip	see **Drink**
scary	see **Frightened**	skip	see **Jump**
scoff	see **Eat**	slave away	see **Work**
scream	see **Call**	sleepy	see **Sleep**
second-hand	see **Old**	sling	see **Throw**
section	see **Part**	slip	see **Give**
see	see **Imagine**	slip	see **Mistake**
see	see **Understand**	slumber	see **Sleep**
seething	see **Angry**	smarmy	see **Friend**
segment	see **Part**	smart	see **Clever**
sense	see **Know**	smirk	see **Smile**
set in motion	see **Start**	smug	see **Proud**
set up	see **Start**	snack	see **Eat**
share out	see **Give**	snag	see **Problem**
shattered	see **Tired**	sneer	see **Smile**
shepherd	see **Take**	snigger	see **Laugh**
shift	see **Move**	snobbish	see **Proud**
shivering	see **Cold**	snooze	see **Sleep**
shocked	see **Surprised**	soaked	see **Wet**
shoplift	see **Steal**	sociable	see **Friend**
shoplifter	see **Steal**	sodden	see **Wet**
shout	see **Call**	soft	see **Quiet**
shriek	see **Call**	solid	see **Real**
shrink	see **Small**	somebody	see **Person**
shrivel	see **Small**	someone	see **Person**
significant	see **Important**	spat	see **Argue**
silent	see **Quiet**	specialist	see **Know**
silly	see **Stupid**	speechless	see **Surprised**
simper	see **Smile**	speedy	see **Fast**
simple	see **Easy**	spicy	see **Hot**

spooky	see **Frightened**
spot	see **Look**
spring	see **Jump**
sprint	see **Run**
spy	see **Look**
squabble	see **Argue**
squirm	see **Move**
stack	see **Put**
staggering	see **Surprised**
stall	see **Stop**
stand	see **Put**
stand by	see **Promise**
standard	see **Ordinary**
stare	see **Look**
stick to	see **Promise**
still	see **Quiet**
stir	see **Move**
straightforward	see **Easy**
streetwise	see **Clever**
strenuous	see **Difficult**
stride	see **Walk**
stroll	see **Walk**
study	see **Look**
stunning	see **Surprised**
subdued	see **Quiet**
success	see **Win**
suitable	see **Right**
sum	see **Money**
summon	see **Call**
superior	see **Proud**
supersonic	see **Fast**

support	see **Carry**
surrounding	see **Near**
survey	see **Ask**
suspect	see **Think**
swallow	see **Drink**
swear	see **Promise**
sweep the board	see **Win**
sweltering	see **Hot**
swig	see **Drink**
swing	see **Move**
synonym	see **Same**

Tt

taciturn	see **Quiet**
take	see **Carry**
taken aback	see **Surprised**
tale	see **Story**
talented	see **Good**
task	see **Job**
tear	see **Run**
tell	see **Say**
tender	see **Love**
terrible	see **Bad**
terribly	see **Very**
terrified	see **Frightened**
the haves	see **Rich**
thick	see **Stupid**
thief	see **Steal**
thrilled	see **Happy**
thunderous	see **Loud**
tiff	see **Argue**

tiny	see **Small**
tip	see **Payment**
tiptoe	see **Walk**
tired out	see **Tired**
titter	see **Laugh**
to be getting on	see **Old**
to be industrious	see **Work**
toil	see **Work**
toss	see **Throw**
tote	see **Carry**
tough	see **Difficult**
tour	see **Travel**
trade	see **Job**
transfer	see **Move**
transport	see **Carry**
transport	see **Move**
transport	see **Take**
treasure	see **Value**
trek	see **Walk**
tricky	see **Difficult**
trip	see **Travel**
triumph	see **Win**
true	see **Real**
truly	see **Very**
typical	see **Ordinary**

Uu

unbolt	see **Open**
uncomplicated	see **Easy**
underprivileged	see **Poor**
undertake	see **Promise**

undertaking	see **Job**
unfold	see **Open**
unforgettable	see **Remember**
unhappy	see **Sad**
unique	see **Different**
unlock	see **Open**
unscrew	see **Open**
unwise	see **Stupid**
unwrap	see **Open**
used	see **Old**
useless	see **Bad**
user-friendly	see **Easy**

Vv

vain	see **Proud**
vary	see **Different**
vault	see **Jump**
verbatim	see **Same**
veteran	see **Old**
victory	see **Win**
vintage	see **Old**
visualise	see **Imagine**
vital	see **Important**
vocation	see **Job**
vow	see **Promise**
voyage	see **Travel**

Ww

| wade | see **Walk** |
| waffle | see **Talk** |

wages	see **Payment**
walkover	see **Win**
wander	see **Travel**
wander	see **Walk**
warm	see **Friend**
warm	see **Hot**
waterlogged	see **Wet**
wealth	see **Money**
wealthy	see **Rich**
weary	see **Tired**
weighty	see **Important**
well-heeled	see **Rich**
well-off	see **Rich**
whim	see **Want**
whisper	see **Say**
wide open	see **Open**
win easily	see **Win**
wisecrack	see **Joke**
wish for	see **Want**
within walking distance	see **Near**
witter	see **Talk**
witty	see **Funny**
wonder	see **Think**
wonderful	see **Good**
word for word	see **Same**
worn out	see **Tired**
worship	see **Love**
worth	see **Value**
wriggle	see **Move**
writhe	see **Move**

Yy

yarn	see **Story**
yearn for	see **Want**
yell	see **Call**

Acknowledgements

The publishers would like to thank the following artists who have contributed to this book:

Lisa Alderson, Julie Banyard, Martin Camm, Jim Channell, Kuo Kang Chen, Mark Davis, Nicholas Forder, Mike Foster, Luigi Gallante, Peter Gregory, Alan Hancocks, Ron Haywood, Sally Holmes, Richard Hook, Rob Jakeway, Tony Kenyon, Sue King, Steve Kirk, Mick Loates, Kevin Madison, Alan Male, Janos Marffy, Josephine Martin, Tracy Morgan, Gill Platt, Terry Riley, Andy Robinson, Mike Saunders, Peter Sarson, Rob Sheffield, Guy Smith, Roger Smith, Mike Taylor, Peter Taylor, Mike White, Colin Woolf

The publishers would like to thank the following for supplying photographs for this book:
Corbis: Reuters New Media 173 (t/l)

All other pictures: Corel, DigitalSTOCK, PhotoDisc